Steelin' Scales and Modes

VOL. 1: The Major Scale and its Modes

for C6 Tuning

by

Mike Neer

Acknowledgments

I would like to extend my gratitude to a few people who, through their influence, help or support, have made this book possible.

To my friends at the Steel Guitar Forum—I've been constantly challenged, enlightened and encouraged by you. Thank you for being such a great community, with special thanks to Bobby Lee (b0b) and Brad Bechtel.

To my steel guitar playing pals, Don Rooke, Tony Locke, Jeremy Wakefield and Lee Jeffriess—steel guitar studs, but even better human beings.

To my pal, Sal Shepherd, who patiently lets me bounce ideas off of him, always with an open ear and a positive outlook.

To some of the great teachers who, even though I never had the opportunity to study with personally, have taught me so much: Lennie Tristano, Charlie Banacos, and Barry Harris—thank you for your dedication to helping others unlock their creative potential.

To my lovely wife, Zoraydee, who is the best person I have ever known.

To my children, Angelica, William, and Michael, Jr.: you have my unconditional love and support in anything you choose to do in life.

Introduction

Music books have always been a source of intrigue for me; as a young boy whose parents couldn't afford music lessons, imagine the joy I felt upon discovering that I could learn things on my own from books! From standing in the sheet music section at the local music store waiting for my cousin to finish his guitar lesson on Saturday mornings, to finding music books in the local library, I became a voracious seeker of knowledge of all things musical. I began to keep my own notebooks, a practice I still use today, and the process of writing the scales and building chords really helped to shape the kind of musician and teacher I would later become.

Years ago, I met another steel player while on break at one of my gigs and we talked shop for a while. He later joked that he didn't know how to play a C major scale in C6. I hadn't attempted playing in C6 yet, so it wasn't until a few years later that I really understood what he was getting at. When I finally decided to learn C6, I remembered that conversation and laughed—I finally got what he was trying to say. I realized that I, too, was beginning to fall into the "position trap". This is one of the things that set me out on a long journey of problem solving for the steel guitar.

I began listening to a ton of steel guitar music, and I realized that I hadn't begun to scratch the surface yet with my playing. This was a great incentive for me, and yet, no matter how many fretboard diagrams I looked at, it still didn't help me see deeper into the tuning. The great players had all figured out their own ways of visualizing the fretboard and played with a sense of freedom—that's what separated the men from the boys. Players like Buddy Emmons, Vance Terry, Joaquin Murphey, Curly Chalker, Tommy Morrell, Maurice Anderson and Jeremy Wakefield have a clear way of making connections on the neck. That is a key point: in order to have freedom on our instrument, we need to come face to face with our limitations. Learning to play scales in every position on the neck is surely one huge step in the right direction. I believe this book will be a big missing piece of the puzzle for many players looking to go deeper.

I am a firm believer in "knowledge equals power," but knowledge alone does not equal good music. Great musicianship is the perfect balance of knowledge and intuition. There are players who are extremely intuitive and lack the fundamental knowledge of music and don't seem to have any difficulties playing beautifully; however, it can only be imagined how much of an impact that a deeper understanding of music could influence a player of that caliber to take his music further.

Looking back, I don't think I could have predicted that I'd be putting my own thoughts into a music book, but I have to say I've been preparing for it my whole life. I present this book in the hopes that the little bit of knowledge I'm passing on reflects the sharing of love for music from my heart and soul to yours.

Mike Neer
New York, NY

Table of Contents

Chapter 1:
An Introduction to
Scales and Modes

Why should I bother to learn the scales and modes all the way up and down the fretboard? Won't it just make me sound like I am playing mechanically and without any feeling? Shouldn't I just stick with playing the melody? Aren't modes just for playing jazz?

These are all legitimate and common questions. My goal in this book is to help you become a better player, period. You will become a better player when you are able to navigate the neck and move effortlessly between scales and keys, and your melodic ability will increase tenfold. Mastering your instrument does not mean that you will automatically become a sterile, technical player; on the contrary, having a clear understanding of all the notes on the neck and how they connect from one key to another, one chord change to another, will increase your ability to pinpoint exactly what you want to play and to more effectively play what you hear in your head. Soon, you will be able to pick melodies effortlessly just using your ear and your knowledge of the relationships of the notes on the neck. It will also do wonders for your improvisation, as you will gain a sense of empowerment in learning structure—the rest is up to you.

For guitarists who are new to C6 tuning, there is often a roadblock that one hits when trying to migrate what he already knows to fit in the tuning. What frequently happens is either that he settles into the "position trap" or abandons the tuning altogether. For those who do stick with it and delve deeply into the tuning, the rewards are great.

As far as music theory is concerned, it is not some dark mystery and it need not be an impediment to one's natural musical intuition; it is simply a way of understanding, communicating and putting a name to things you may already know. For those who already have a grasp on these elements of music theory, you will find new ways of putting to use what you know and hopefully discover things you didn't know. For those of you who aren't interested in the nuts and bolts of it all, go ahead and skip to Chapter 2. This will all still be here when you need it.

The focus of this is getting you to learn and play all of your scales and modes. You will not need to know any music theory to benefit from this book, but if you *really* want to reap the rewards, then I highly suggest studying the basic fundamentals of music theory. I will be introducing some very important points here, but you should make it a point to seek out other resources for more in-depth studies. The focus of this book will be narrow in scope compared to the vast universe of information.

Things we will be talking about:

- Key signatures and reading notes on the staff
- The Circle of Fifths
- Tetrachords
- Modes and the relationships of scales to each other
- An introduction to Chord/scale theory

Most importantly, in this book I will be introducing a new concept called the "Tetrachord System." This is a system of looking at scales in a whole new way, one that never occurred to me in all of my years of playing music until I became hooked on playing steel guitar. It's only recently that I have committed much of my time and energy into developing this—I did it as a way of improving my own playing and I think it has helped me immensely.

There is a lot of material contained in this book, and much of it is repetition designed solely to help you memorize all of the formulae for building scales anywhere on your instrument. Patience and perseverance will serve you well here, because in the end, when all of the pieces of the puzzle fit together, you will see and hear the difference in your playing

Reading Notes on the Staff

Knowing the notes on your guitar is not enough; you will need to learn to read the notes on the staff as well.

The staff consists of five lines; notes appear both on the lines and in the spaces.

The symbol on the left is called the "*treble clef*", followed by the time signature. The treble clef covers notes that are above "middle C". In this book, we will only cover notes on the treble clef.

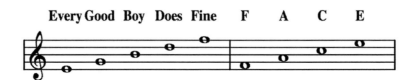

Use the phrases above to help memorize the note names. Ledger lines are used when notes extend beyond the range of the five staff lines, both above and below. If we extend the notes on the staff lines to ledger lines, this is how the notes are spelled:

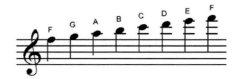

It is important to familiarize yourself with the layout of the staff.

Another crucial area that will need your immediate attention is the matter of *key signatures*. The key signature will tell you what key the music is written in, and the sharps or flats in the key signature itself affect how the notes on the staff are read. The key signature makes it possible to avoid having sharps or flats in each instance of certain notes.

 This is the key signature for A Major. The sharps (#) that fall on the lines and in the spaces change the value of those notes for the duration, unless they are temporarily overruled by a natural sign. The natural before the F (image below) indicates that it will be an F natural until the next measure or it is made sharp again.

Circle of Fifths
of
Major Keys

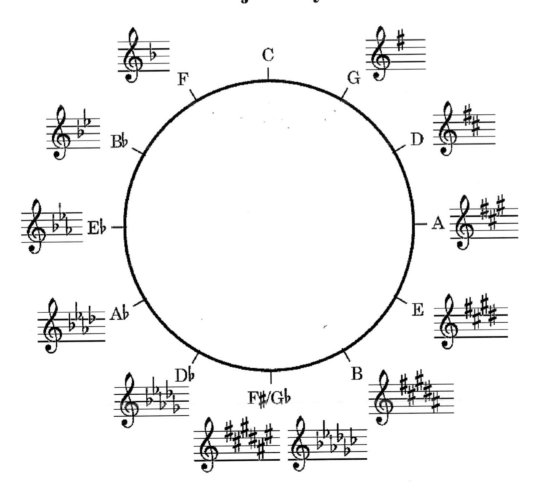

This is an image you will be referring back to often; this diagram will play an important role in your understanding of some of the principles and concepts applied in this book.

The Major Scale

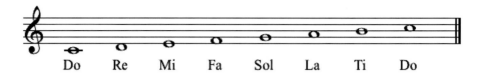

Do   Re   Mi   Fa   Sol   La   Ti   Do

I'm sure you remember Julie Andrews in *The Sound of Music* singing "Do Re Mi":

Doe, a deer, a female deer,
Ray, a drop of golden sun....

Depending on your age, that may have been your first introduction to the major scale—I'm certain it was mine.

So, what's the big deal about scales, anyway?   Scales are the most important elements in Western music, as they are our sources of harmony and melody. The *diatonic scale*, also known as the *major* or *natural minor* scale, contains seven notes (*degrees*) and repeats itself at the octave.

The notes of a scale are arranged according to pitch—ascending scales increase in pitch, descending scales decrease in pitch. Some scales have different note values as they ascend and descend (melodic minor). In addition to the diatonic scales, there are many other scales, such as the chromatic scale (12 notes), the whole tone scale (six notes), the harmonic minor and melodic minor scales (seven notes), the pentatonic scale (five notes), and the diminished scale (eight notes). I will cover these other scales in-depth in a subsequent volume of this book.

Every scale of a particular type has the exact same construction, just using different pitches, so what applies to one major scale applies to all the others, as well. The same goes for harmonic and melodic minor.

Tetrachords

The diatonic major scales and minor scales (natural, harmonic and melodic) are each composed of seven notes, not including the octave. The inclusion of the octave gives us eight notes, so we can then divide the scales into two equal parts, called *tetrachords*. The tetrachord is at the heart of what makes this book work and my discovery and application of it with regard to the C6 tuning has made it possible for me to obtain a greater degree of freedom in improvisation and melody playing, in general.

A tetrachord is simply four consecutive scale tones. An important feature of a tetrachord is that *it encompasses the range of a perfect 4th.*

You can see the scale above divided into two tetrachords: the C Ionian tetrachord (the *lower tetrachord*) and the G Ionian tetrachord (the *upper tetrachord*). Both of these tetrachords are identical in terms of construction: **Tone – Tone – Semitone**, separated by a tone (which we do not count because each of those two degrees, F and G, belong to separate tetrachords).

In our diatonic scales, there are four tetrachords types: *Ionian, Dorian, Phrygian,* and *Lydian*. These also happen to be the names of the first four modes of the diatonic scale. Take a look at the tetrachord formulas (*Note: T = tone and S = semitone*):

Tetrachord	Formula
Ionian	T- T- S *or* 2- 2- 1
Dorian	T- S -T *or* 2- 1- 2
Phrygian	S- T- T *or* 1- 2- 2
Lydian	T- T- T *or* 2- 2- 2

Before we go any further with the tetrachords and their Greek names, let's have a look at where these names come from: the modes of the major scales. A quick and simple point about *modes*: the modes of any major scales are all derived from that scale's degrees, and each mode begins on a different scale degree. Each mode takes a different scale degree as its tonic.

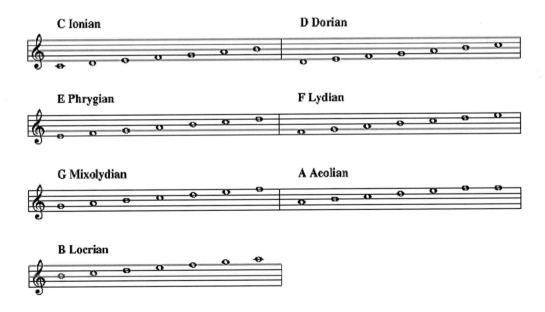

If you look at all seven modes above, you'll see that they all contain the same notes—the notes of the C Major scale. Here is a description for each of the modes:

Mode	Starting note	Scale properties	Quality
Ionian	Tonic	The tonic major scale	Major
Dorian	2nd	Minor 3rd, natural 6th and minor 7th	Minor
Phrygian	3rd	Minor 2nd, minor 6th and minor7th	Minor
Lydian	4th	Major scale with a #4	Major
Mixolydian	5th	Major scale with a minor 7th	Major
Aeolian	6th	Minor 3rd, minor 6th, minor 7th	Minor (relative)
Locrian	7th	Minor 2nd, dim. 5th and minor 7th	Minor

Now that you've read the descriptions of the modes and have a little more knowledge, have a look at the following table, which illustrates the construction of each of the C Major modes in tetrachords:

C Major Modes	Tetrachord 1	Tetrachord 2
C Ionian (major tonality)	C D E F (C Ionian)	G A B C (G Ionian)
D Dorian (minor tonality)	D E F G (D Dorian)	A B C D (A Dorian)
E Phrygian (minor tonality)	E F G A (E Phrygian)	B C D E (B Phrygian)
F Lydian (major tonality)	F G A B (F Lydian)	C D E F (C Ionian)
G Mixolydian (major tonality)	G A B C (G Ionian)	D E F G (D Dorian)
A Aeolian (minor tonality)	A B C D (A Dorian)	E F G A (E Phrygian)
B Locrian (minor tonality)	B C D E (B Phrygian)	F G A B (F Lydian)

As you scan down the left column, you see that the C major scale is spelled out in order from C to B. Columns 2 and 3 illustrate the combination of tetrachords that make up each mode. Again, *we can think of this all as the C Major scale beginning on each scale degree if we like*, so in any situation where you would play notes from the C Major scale, you can play any of these modes. Our ears will guide us as to which notes correspond to the given chords.

You will also notice the tonality of each of the modes—this corresponds to what we know about the diatonic harmony. I'd like to talk about diatonic harmony for a moment.

Diatonic Harmony

Chords are built from the diatonic scale by stacking thirds on top of each chord's root. This is called *tertian* harmony—a third is essentially every other scale tone, so when building chords, we skip a note each time we add a note (the chords are either on the staff lines or in the spaces, not both). This does not apply to inversions, which is for another discussion.

All diatonic harmony built from the major scale has this exact harmonic structure, just with different pitches. We can group the triads into :

- *(3) Major triads*
- *(3) minor triads*
- *(1) diminished chord* (qualifies as minor).

When we stack another third on each of the chords, it really defines the harmony of the scale and introduces a sense of tension and resolution.

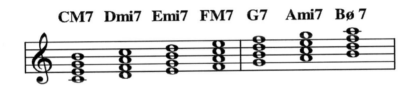

The G7 (V7) and Bø7 (vii7) chords have the greatest need for resolution and, thus, the greatest amount of tension. The CM7 (IM7), Emi7 (iii7) and Ami7 (vi7) are the most consonant, or pleasing.

As we get further into learning the scales, we will use various chord progressions to demonstrate how the chord/scale theory can be a good starting point in improvising.

Intervals

The smallest unit of measurement in harmony is the *interval*. An interval is the measurement of the distance between two notes, expressed in *semitones* and *tones* or half-steps and whole steps. We measure from the lower note to the higher note, with the smallest unit of measure being a semitone. A semitone is the equivalent of one fret on a guitar, or the distance between a black key on a piano to the next white key above it. A tone is equal to two semitones.

When two notes are sounded simultaneously, this is considered a *harmonic interval*; likewise, when notes are sounded consecutively, it is considered a *melodic interval*. In this book, a large majority of what we will be dealing with is the melodic interval.

When we express the values of intervals, we use ordinal numbers (4th, 5th, etc.) the only exceptions being unison and octaves. The ordinal numbers identify the size of the interval, which can range anywhere from a unison to a fifteenth (the double octave); however, these designations do not tell the whole story—there is also the matter of the quality of the interval, which we will get to.

In the diatonic major scale, the intervals between the tonic and all the degrees are considered to *natural* since they are naturally occurring in the diatonic scale. The natural intervals are defined as major and perfect intervals. Perfect intervals are considered to be very consonant, and when they are inverted, they are still perfect. Only the tonic, 4th, 5th and octave are perfect intervals When the 4th is inverted it becomes the 5th and vice versa. The table below illustrates the relationship between the tonic and the other degrees of the diatonic scale:

Tonic	C	C	C	C	C	C	C	C
Scale degree	C	D	E	F	G	A	B	C
Interval	P1 or unison	M2	M3	P4	P5	M6	M7	P8 or octave

In the table above, P stands for perfect and the M for major. Again, the *perfect interval* is considered to be consonant, meaning that its sound is pleasing. The unison, octave, perfect fourth and perfect fifth intervals can be altered, however, to a more dissonant sound. These alterations are *diminished* (lowered by a semitone) and *augmented* (raised by a semitone). Any intervals in our scale can be augmented and all but the tonic can be. Any major interval can be lowered a semitone to a *minor interval* or raised to an *augmented interval*.

Unlike when comparing the scale degrees to the tonic, when scale degrees are measured against each other, we begin to see more of these altered intervallic relationships. For example, when comparing the second degree, D, to the fourth degree, F, we have a distance of three semitones, which is equal to a minor third.

Counting Intervals

Let's take a look at how we count intervals:

1. The first step is to determine the basic interval. We do this simply by counting from the lowest note of our pair to the higher note, giving each note the value of "1". The starting note is 1 and each subsequent note we skip adds on to the total. Here are a few examples:
   - C to E = C D E, or 1 2 3, so the basic interval is a third
   - E to C = E F G A B C, or 1 2 3 4 5 6, so the basic interval is a sixth
   - F to C = F G A B C, or 1 2 3 4 5, so the basic interval is a fifth

2. The second step is to determine the quality of the interval. It makes life a lot easier at this point if one is familiar with all of the 13 Major key signature tonics (refer back to the Circle of Fifths on page 4)—in fact, it is *essential* to learn the key signatures; even on the bandstand, musicians will use fingers pointed up or down to call out keys for tunes. By knowing the key signatures, we could simply refer to the lowest note as the tonic, and then determine whether the higher note is contained within *its* diatonic scale. The following graphics illustrates all the intervals from the m2 to the M9 (m=minor, M=major, P =perfect):

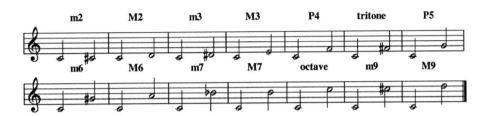

It is difficult to identify the quality of the interval without knowing the key signatures; however, we can count the number of semitones and make an easy determination from that. The following table attempts to illustrate this—look carefully at the left column:

Number of semitones	Major, minor or perfect intervals	Abbr.	Augmented and Diminished intervals	Abbr.
0	Perfect unison	P1		
1	Minor second	m2	Augmented unison	A1
2	Major second	M2		
3	Minor third	m3	Augmented second	A2
4	Major third	M3	Diminished fourth	d4
5	Perfect fourth	P4		
6			Tritone or Aug. fourth, Diminished fifth	A4 d5
7	Perfect fifth	P5		
8	Minor sixth	m6	Augmented fifth	A5
9	Major sixth	M6		
10	Minor seventh	m7	Augmented sixth	A6
11	Major seventh	M7	Diminished octave	d8
12	Perfect octave	P8		

As you can see, it is possible to identify an interval by counting the number of semitones and memorizing the table above. I find it more useful in the bigger picture, however, to simply learn all of the key signatures and use that method, as shown in the previous example. There is plenty of information here to think about, so absorb a little at a time until it becomes part of your practical knowledge.

Chapter 2:
The Major Scales

The following pages will present the Major scales in every key, beginning with the scales from tonic to tonic (Ionian mode) in each of two string sets (2, 3 and 4 and 3, 4 and 5). After we have covered that basic introduction to the scales and the tetrachord formation, we will begin playing the scales starting on each individual scale degree, serving as our introduction to the modes.

Earlier in the book, you read about the four tetrachord shapes (Ionian, Dorian, Phrygian and Lydian) and now we will begin to put them to use. In this chapter, we will focus on the major scales in all keys, from tonic to tonic, on two string sets of three strings (strings 2, 3 and 4 and strings 3, 4 and 5), using simply the Ionian tetrachords. You will discover that each major scale is composed of two tetrachords—one beginning on the the tonic and one beigonning on the 5th. This is the concept of the Tetrachord System—to understand the construction of each and every scale and mode using two tetrachords. It seems like a lot to digest, and it is, but like any big meal, you'll want to take small bites and pace yourself.

I know that you will see the value in learning this system, but it may not be completely apparent at first. It is important to remember that the system itself is not a method for learning how to play music, but it is simply a method for learning how to play your instrument and gaining more freedom in knowing where everything exists on the C6 neck.

A few notes on the way this book has been laid out: First, you will see that I have only used a 6 string neck diagram beginning with a high E string. In any C6 tuning, whether on 8 strings, 6 strings, pedal steel, non-pedal steel, or any other variation of the tuning, such as C6/A7 or C13 or with a high G string in the first string slot, the foundation of the tuning lies in the strings 1-5 as shown in the diagram. Being that this is the case and that it would also be a monumental task of allowing for every variation of this foundation, I have chosen to focus on the two string sets mentioned above. If your guitar is tuned in such a way that allows you to expand this concept on your instrument, then you should make it a priority to do so after the basic positions have been mastered here.

The crux of this book is the division of the scales into tetrachords. By doing so, we are able to take advantage of playing up and down the neck using similar, if not exact, shapes. This gives us greater flexibility in playing in any key in any position on the neck and, as you will see for yourself, really expands our As an added benefit Also, our picking gains a greater sense of articulation when we are playing more up and down the strings and less across the strings.

All scales appear on the diagrams beginning with the lowest possible tetrachord in the string set. In some cases, the root tetrachord is *not* the lowest possible tetrachord, so I have included those lower tetrachords as hollowed out markers. It is important to learn all of the positions for each key, as later on we will be combining string sets. **An important point to note is that if you are playing a tetrachord below the tonic tetrachord, the root will repeat—therefor, it is necessary to leave out the root note of the lower tetrachord when playing an ascending scale, or else the root note will be doubled. Conversely, when descending, we eliminate the root note from the upper tetrachord.**

We will begin with the Major scale divided into two symmetrical Ionian tetrachords (2 2 1) on string set 234. Our keys are laid out in accordance with the Circle of Fifths. The only key signatures here with enharmonic equivalents are F# and Gb—C# and Cb are so uncommonly used that I will not even list them here.

Take your time learning the scales—you must be completely comfortable with the Ionian tetrachords in all keys on both string sets before moving on. It's important to realize that this is part of a process that takes a considerable amount of time to become a part of your playing, but if one is diligent in learning these and committing them to memory, I believe the process will move along much more quickly and the Tetrachord System will become a part of your playing.

A few quick notes…

On the neck diagrams, all scales are laid out from lower tetrachord to upper tetrachord, in that order, in black dots. When you see white markes on the frets below the black dots, that is simply to bring some of the lower notes into play, since the scale begins at a very high fret. In those cases, when playing the upper tetrachord voiced below the lower tetrachord, it is important to avoid repeating the tonic note, since both tetracvhords contain that note.

Second, you will see symbols inside of the fret markers—these are the scale intervals.

- R = root
- p = perfect
- Δ = Major
- ♭ = a flatted, or minor degree

MAJOR SCALES
IONIAN TETRACHORDS
(string set 2,3,4)

C Major Scale

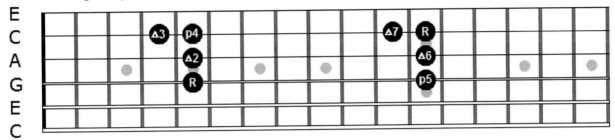

G Major scale

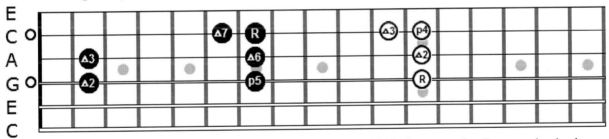

Note that in the case of G major, the lowest possible note on string set 234 is the open string G, so we simply change the shape using the open strings. This shape is not practical up and down the neck, so we will use it only in this case.

D Major scale

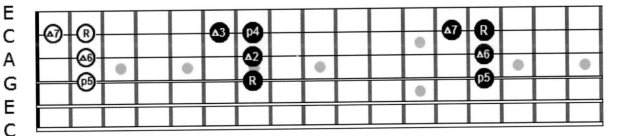

A Major scale

A Ionian Tetrachord   E Ionian Tetrachord

A Major (A Ionian + E Ionian) string set 234

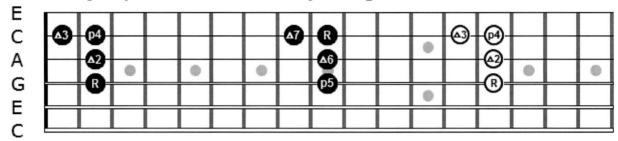

E Major scale

E Ionian Tetrachord   B Ionian Tetrachord

E Major (E Ionian + B Ionian) string set 234

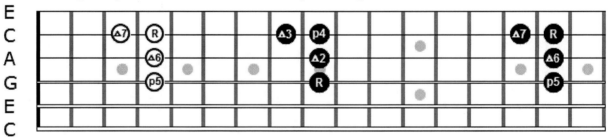

B Major Scale

B Ionian Tetrachord   F#Ionian Tetrachord

B Major (B Ionian + F# Ionian) string set 234

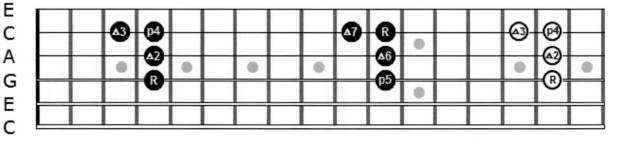

15

F# Major scale

F# Ionian Tetrachord   C# Ionian Tetrachord

Gb Major scale

Gb Ionian Tetrachord   Db Ionian Tetrachord

Gb or F# Major (Gb Ionian + Db Ionian) string set 234

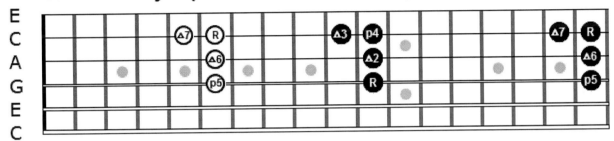

Db Major scale

Db Ionian Tetrachord   Ab Ionian Tetrachord

Db Major (Db Ionian + Ab Ionian) string set 234

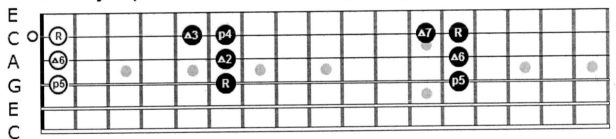

Ab Major scale

Ab Ionian Tetrachord   Eb Ionian Tetrachord

Ab Major (Ab Ionian + Eb Ionian) string set 234

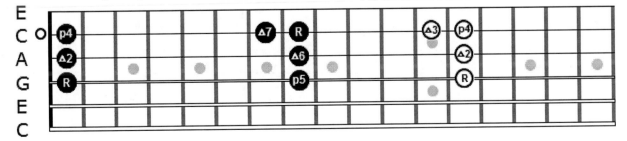

Eb Major scale

Eb Ionian Tetrachord   Bb Ionian Tetrachord

Eb Major (Eb Ionian + Bb Ionian) string set 234

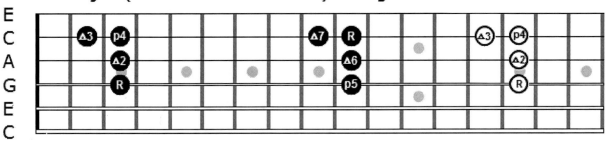

Bb Major scale

Bb Ionian Tetrachord   F Ionian Tetrachord

Bb Major (Bb Ionian + F Ionian) string set 234

F Major scale

F Ionian Tetrachord   C Ionian Tetrachord

F Major (F Ionian + C Ionian) string set 234

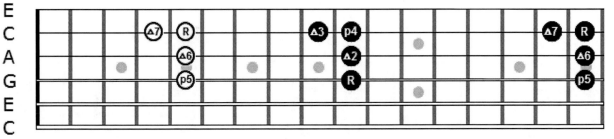

17

IONIAN TETRACHORDS
(string set 3,4,5)

C Major scale

C Major (C Ionian + G Ionian) string set 345

G Major scale

G Major (G Ionian + D Ionian) string set 345

D Major scale

D Major (D Ionian + A Ionian) string set 345

A Major scale

A Major (A Ionian + E Ionian) string set 345

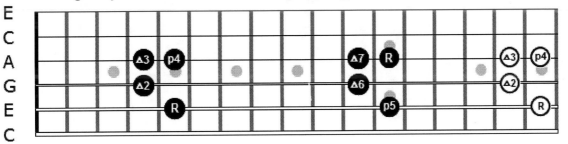

E Major scale

E Major (E Ionian + B Ionian) string set 345

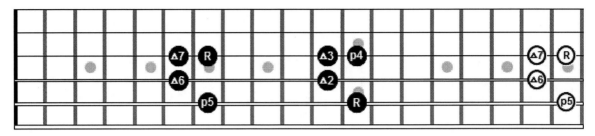

B Major scale

B Major (B Ionian + F# Ionian) string set 345

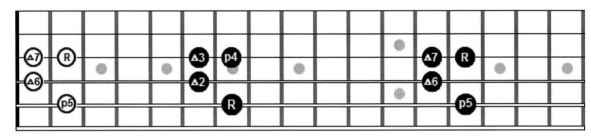

F# Major or Gb Major scale

F# Major (F# Ionian + C# Ionian) string set 345

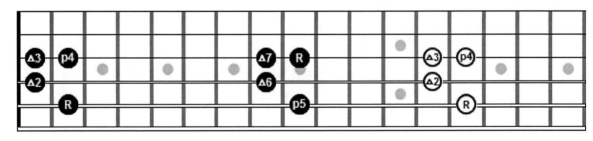

Db Major scale

Db Major (Db Ionian + Ab Ionian) string set 345

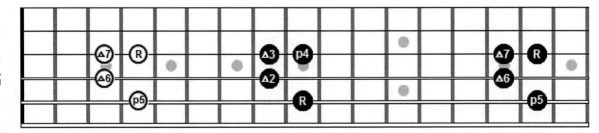

Ab Major scale

Ab Major (Ab Ionian + Eb Ionian) string set 345

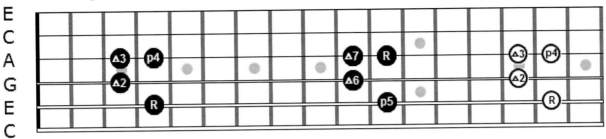

Eb Major scale

Eb Major (Eb Ionian + Bb Ionian) string set 345

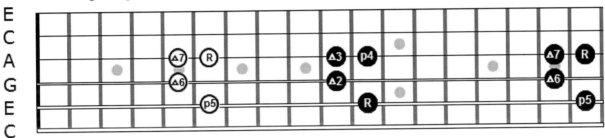

Bb Major scale

Bb Major (Bb Ionian + F Ionian) string set 345

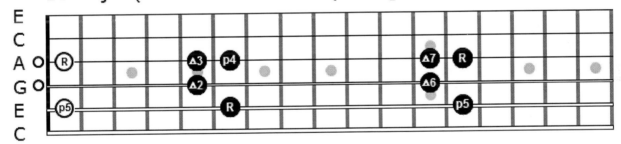

F Major scale

F Major (F Ionian + C Ionian) string set 345

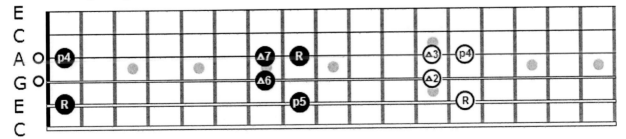

IONIAN TETRACHORDS
(COMBINED STRING SETS)

In this section, we look at combining the string sets in order to extend the range of our scales, but more importantly reduce the length of travel from one tetrachord to the next. For the sake avoiding confusion, we will only use the tonic tetrachord on string set 345 and the 5th tetrachord on string set 234.

The limitation of range, or the high position of some of these scales may seem a bit problematic, but I will introduce a workaround for that a bit later.

It is important at this time to just stick with the scale patterns I am presenting in this order. I know it may seem that in some cases what has been presented may not be a logical choice, but it will start to make sense as we progress further. The object is really just to embed the tetrachord shapes in your mind so that their recall will become second nature. That is the beauty of this system—the pieces fit together like a jigsaw puzzle, but one that takes more than just a rainy afternoon.

C Major scale

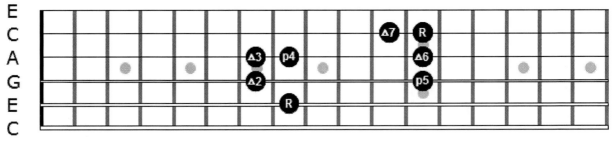

G Major scale

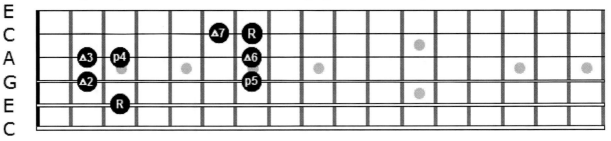

D Major scale

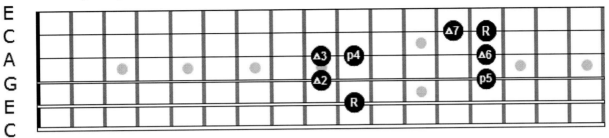

D Major (D Ionian + A Ionian) (Combined)

A major scale

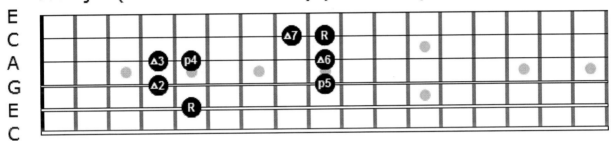

A Major (A Ionian + E Ionian) (Combined)

E Major scale

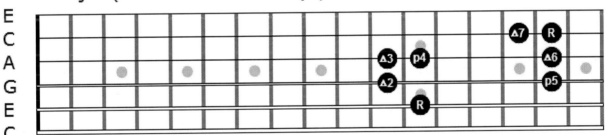

E Major (E Ionian + B Ionian) (Combined)

B Major scale

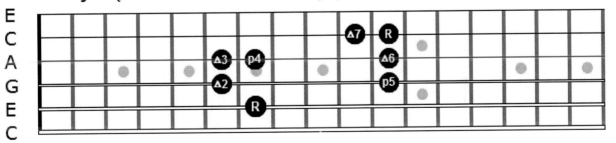

B Major (B Ionian + F# Ionian) (Combined)

F# or Gb Major scale

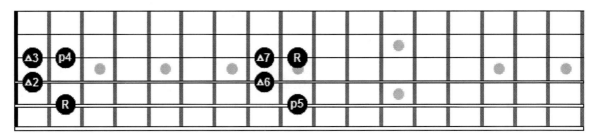

F# Major (F# Ionian + C# Ionian) (Combined)

Db or C# Major scale

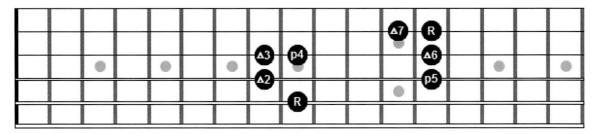

Db Major (Db Ionian + Ab Ionian) (Combined)

Ab Major scale

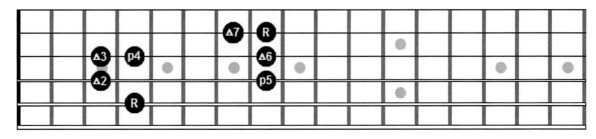

Ab Major (Ab Ionian + Eb Ionian) (Combined)

Eb Major scale

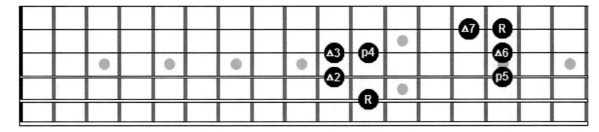

Eb Major (Eb Ionian + Bb Ionian) (Combined)

Bb Major scale

Bb Major (Bb Ionian + F Ionian) (Combined)

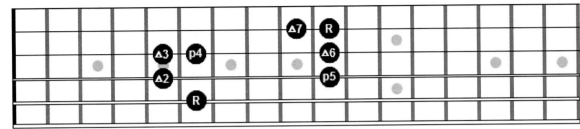

F Major scale

F Major (F Ionian + C Ionian) (Combined)

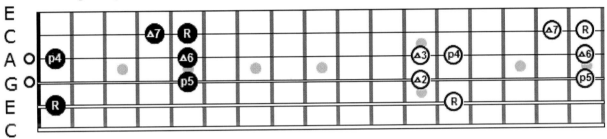

Chapter 3:
The Modes
of the Major Scale

In chapter 3 we will be taking a look at the remaining tetrachord shapes for the diatonic scale, and in doing so will begin our study of the major scale modes.

In the short term, we can look at these diagrams as a means of learning how to play our scales beginning with any note of the scale, and the availability of all the tetrachord shapes gives us the ability to connect them up and down the neck. It is truly liberating to have this ability to connect your ideas seamlessly, as you will no doubt discover.

You may also discover that there are more ways to play than to just limit yourself to the Tetrachord System, and this is absolutely true. But the one thing I can say to you is that using the Tetrachord System will help you learn your scales in every position more quickly and efficiently than any other system available. It was strictly designed by myself for this purpose. As I've said earlier, and as I will repeat frequently as personal trainer does to a client for motivation, *you will own the neck and gain complete command of it*. It is entirely up to you to be as musical as possible, a journey which should last an entire lifetime, and learning the neck gives you a clear advantage.

We will begin by looking at the remaining tetrachord shapes before moving into modal territory. For a refresher, here are the two Ionian tetrachord shapes we've studied up until this point:

Ionian tetrachords on 2 string sets

These should just about be second nature to you now and you should be able to play all the major scales using either one or both of these shapes.

What are Modes?

The most common questions about modes are "*Just what exactly are modes?*", "*What purpose do modes serve?*" and "*How do I put modes to use?*" I think it's only wise that before we move into the modal territory I should try to clear up a few things about modes.

Modes are scales derived from a parent scale using a different tonic, thereby creating an alternate tonality for that scale. In the simplest example I can think of, here is one way that you've been playing with modes and may not have even been aware: *playing the Blues*.

Let's look at a 12-bar Blues in the key of C:

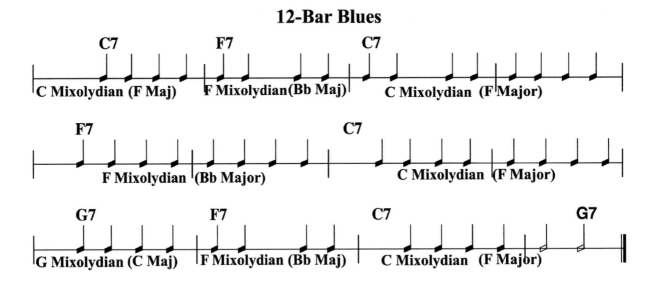

12-Bar Blues

Looking at the 12-Bar Blues above, you will see the modes/scales that correspond to the chord changes below the rhythm line. As you may have notice, even though this is a blues in C, the parent scale of the C Mixolydian, which is what we would use for a dominant 7th sound, is F Major. This is how we begin to understand how modes work.

Let's take, for example, a harmonica player—in order for him or her to play a blues in C, she would need to use the cross harp technique, but to do so, she'd have to select a harmonica that would be in the appropriate key for playing blues. The harmonica player would select an F diatonic harp and use the draw notes to bend accordingly. This is modal thinking, although you will rarely hear it referred to as such.

In continuing to look at the example, for each dominant chord we are playing a Mixolydian mode from a parent key one 5th below. Taking a close look at the changes of a tune is how we are able to determine the functions of chords and make the appropriate choices for improvisation, although "appropriate" is a very suggestive term. However, this is a good framework to get started with.

We've already stated that the key is C, and the I chord is C7. Based on what we know about diatonic harmony, we know that there is only one dominant chord in each diatonic scale, and that dominant chord is based on the 5th degree of thescale. There is no C7 in the key of C, so the C7 chord belongs to another diatonic scale: F Major. How is it possible that the Blues in C is really the Blues in F Major? Well, it's very simple: the mode of the F Major scale that supplies the C7 is the 5th mode, or the Mixolydian mode. In essence, we will play the notes of the F Major scale (C Mixolydian) over our C7. What knowledge of the modes does for us, however, is gives us the tonal center with which to concentrate over our specific chords—for C7, we want to focus on those chord tones, rather than just randomly playing the F Major scale.

There are many more examples of how modes come into play. One of the crucial steps in playing music is in understanding the functions of chords. If we look at another example, we will see that even though a chord exists in the diatonic harmony, its particular function may be different in the scheme of the chord progression than it would normally be in diatonic situations. A perfect example is a iii-VI7-ii-V7 turnaround. If we think in the key of C, our turnaround would be:

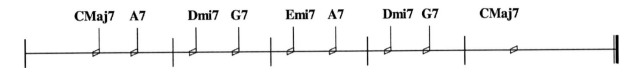

As you can see, there are chords that are diatonic to the key of C, and some that are not. A7 is the first we encounter, and as you can surmise, we are playing an A Mixolydian there, which belongs to the parent scale D Major. When we get to bar 3, you see Emi7—this happens to be diatonic to C as the Phrygian, but since it is moving to a dominant chord (A7), I'd prefer to look at it as the ii7 in the key D, giving us E Dorian. That whole 3rd measure we are temporarily playing in the key of D. Try and see if you can wrap your head around a few more examples. It is a difficult concept to get in the beginning

THE DORIAN MODE

Let's look at the 2nd mode of the major scale, the *Dorian mode*. As discussed earlier, the Dorian mode begins on the second degree of a major scale, so the second degree becomes the tonic. The main property of the Dorian mode is that it is a minor scale with a minor 7th.

D Dorian

Being that the root of this mode is D, we have to compare it with the D Major scale in order to define its properties.

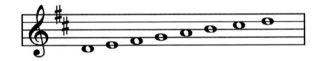

The key signature shows the D Major scale has an F# and a C#, but the D Dorian, derived from the C Major scale, has neither. At this time, we can view the D Dorian as a way of playing the C scale from its 2nd degree—it is diatonic to the C scale, and its tonic harmony, Dmin7, serves as the ii7, or supertonic 7th chord in C.

We have the option of playing the Dorian tetrachord in two shapes:

Dorian tetrachord, string set 234, b3 option

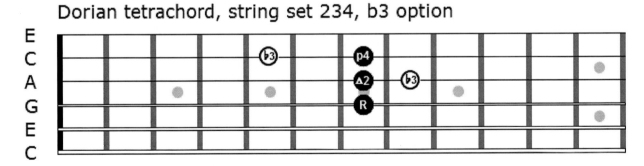

I refer to the first shape as Type 1 (b3 on the 2nd string) and the second as Type 2. Certain situations call for the use of one over the other, but for certain reasons I often prefer Type 1 and use it most often in this text. If you disagree, then by all means, go with what suits you better. After all, it is about your internalization of the information.

DORIAN TETRACHORDS
(string set 2, 3, 4)

D Dorian mode

D Dorian (D Dorian + A Dorian) string set 234

A Dorian mode

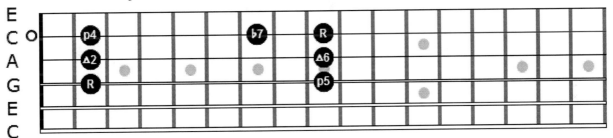

A Dorian (A Dorian + E Dorian) string set 234

E Dorian mode

E Dorian (E Dorian + B Dorian) string set 234

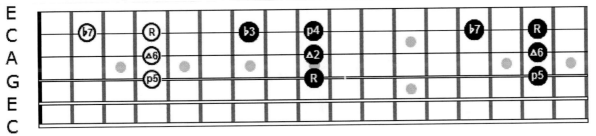

B Dorian mode

B Dorian (B Dorian + F# Dorian) string set 234

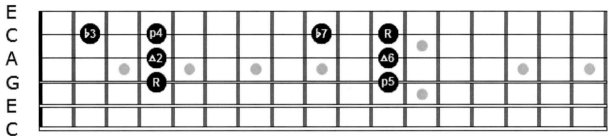

F# Dorian mode

F# Dorian (F# Dorian + C# Dorian) string set 234

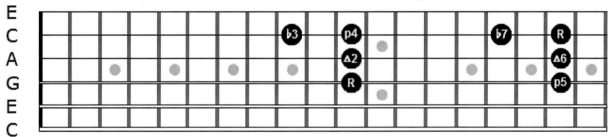

C# Dorian mode

C# Dorian (C# Dorian + G# Dorian) string set 234

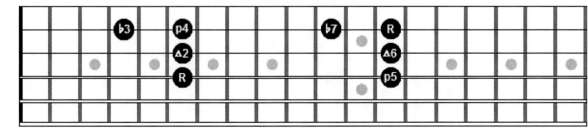

G# Dorian or Ab Dorian mode

G# (Ab) Dorian (G# (Ab) Dorian + D# (Eb) Dorian) string set 234

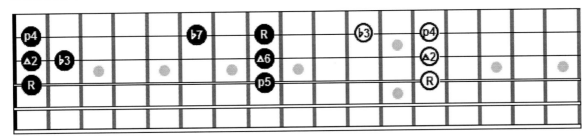

Note the use of the Type 2 Dorian tetrachord shape at the first fret.

Eb Dorian mode

Eb Dorian (Eb Dorian + Bb Dorian) string set 234

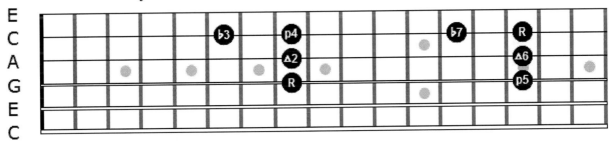

Bb Dorian mode

Bb Dorian (Bb Dorian + F Dorian) string set 234

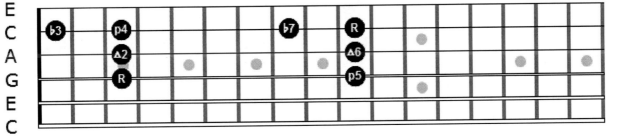

F Dorian mode

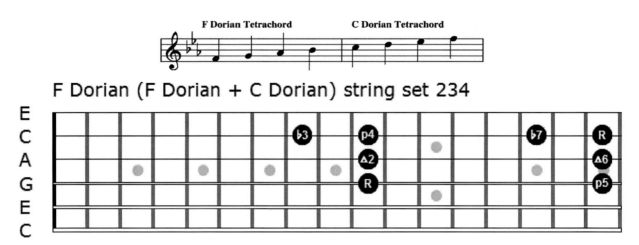

F Dorian (F Dorian + C Dorian) string set 234

C Dorian mode

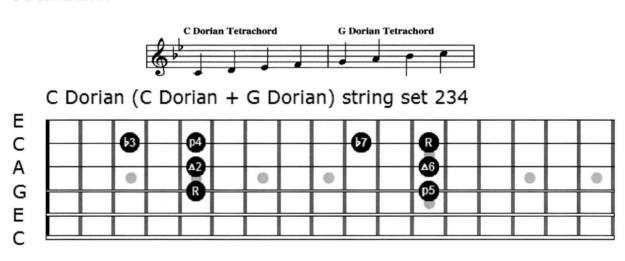

C Dorian (C Dorian + G Dorian) string set 234

G Dorian mode

G Dorian (G Dorian + D Dorian) string set 234

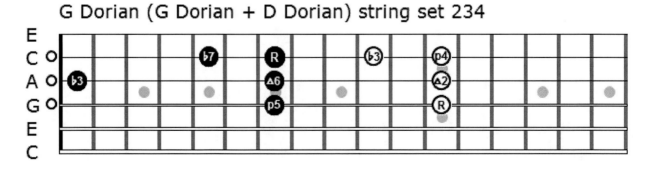

Note the use of the second Dorian tetrachord shape in the open strings.

DORIAN TETRACHORDS
(string set 3, 4, 5)

D Dorian mode

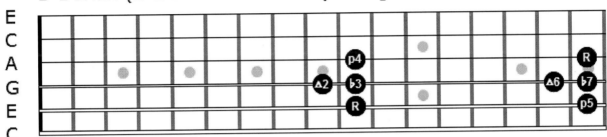

A Dorian mode

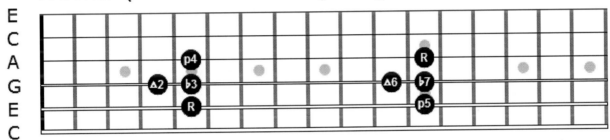

E Dorian mode

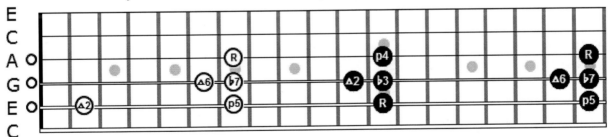

Note the first tonic tetrachord using open strings—the shape had to be changed for that tetrachord, but it still very playable.

B Dorian mode

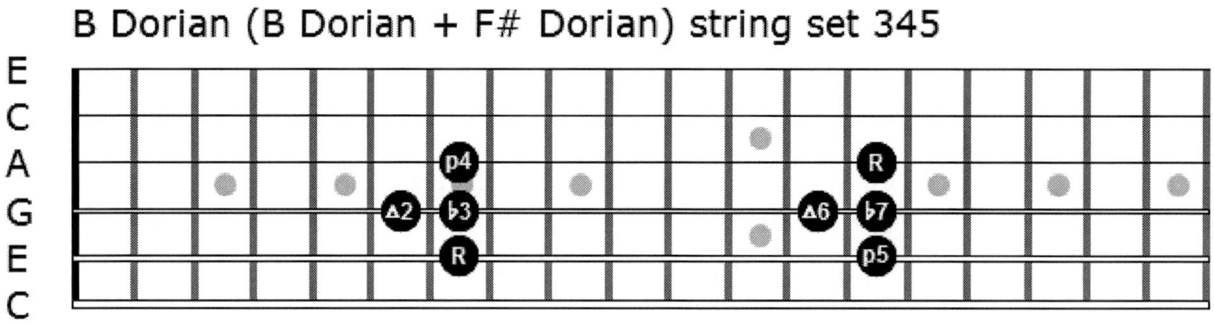

B Dorian (B Dorian + F# Dorian) string set 345

F# Dorian mode

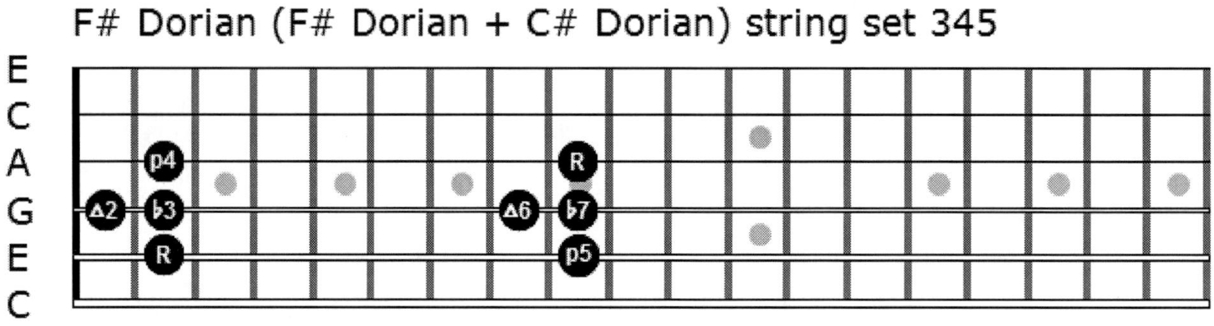

F# Dorian (F# Dorian + C# Dorian) string set 345

C# Dorian mode

C# Dorian (C# Dorian + G# Dorian) string set 345

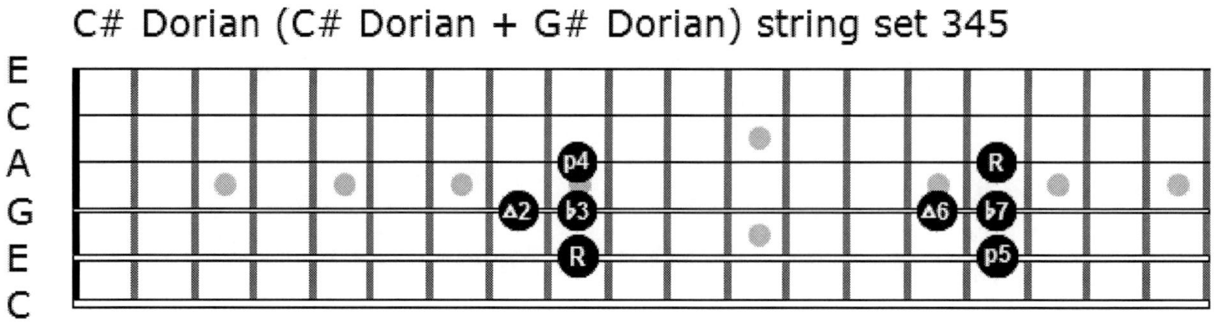

G# Dorian or Ab Dorian mode

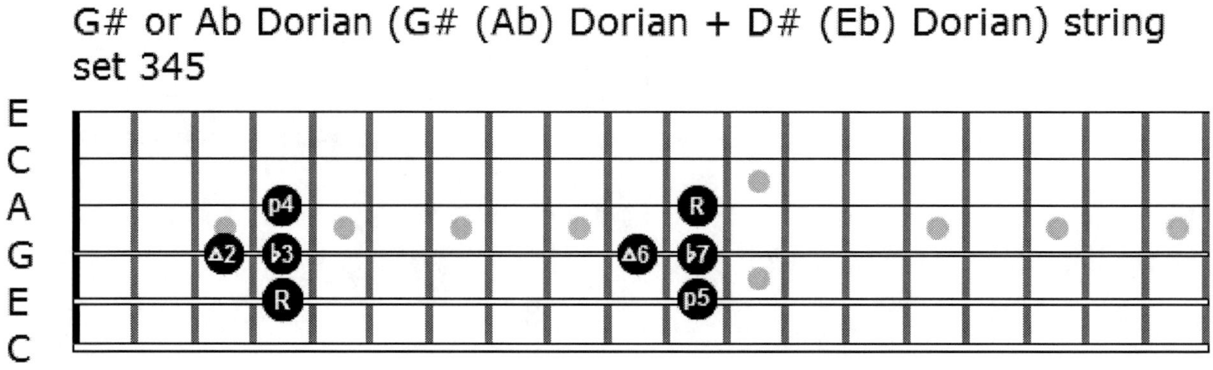

G# or Ab Dorian (G# (Ab) Dorian + D# (Eb) Dorian) string set 345

Eb Dorian mode

Eb Dorian (Eb Dorian + Bb Dorian) string set 345

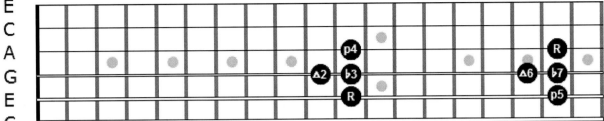

Bb Dorian mode

Bb Dorian (Bb Dorian + F Dorian) string set 345

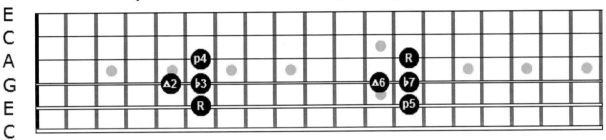

F Dorian mode

F Dorian (F Dorian + C Dorian) string set 345

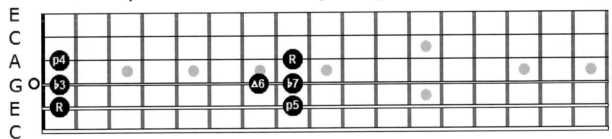

C Dorian mode

C Dorian (C Dorian + G Dorian) string set 345

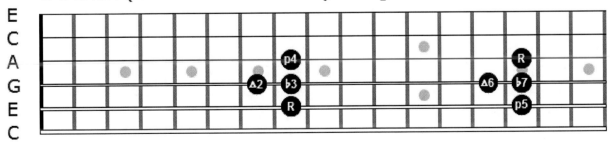

G Dorian (G Dorian + D Dorian) string set 345

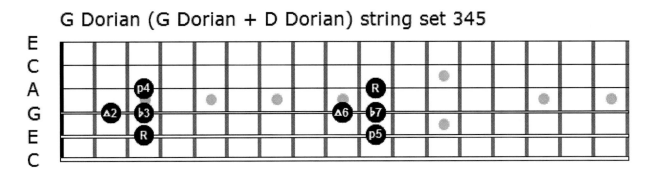

EXERCISES
Ionian and Dorian modes

With the first two modes (Ionian and Dorian) of the major scale under our bar, we can begin to link them together and hear the different sounds we can get. Our upper and lower tetrachords will have different sounds than each other.

I've used the other Dorian shape in this example, as you can see it more clearly. Have a look at the two lower tetrachords—the C Ionian and the D Dorian. The range of the two combined covers a 5th—from C to G—not a complete octave, but it is enough to strongly define a sound. If you look at the upper tetrachords, you'll find a note grouping ranging from the 5th (G) to the 9th (D). There is no F contained in the upper tetrachords, so if we were to use that position to play over a Dmi7 vamp, such as Miles Davis's "So What", we'd have a very nice, open modal sound. This would also be great to play over a D9sus, or similar chords, as heard in many great '60s and '70s Jazz recordings, such as "Maiden Voyage".

C Ionian + D Dorian--strings 234

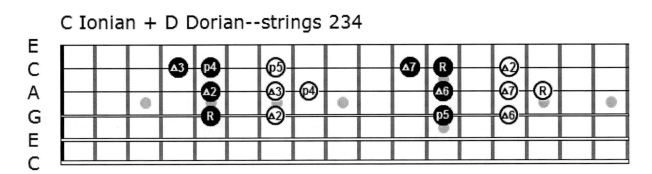

Let's look at the same two modes on strings 345:

C Ionian + D Dorian--strings 345

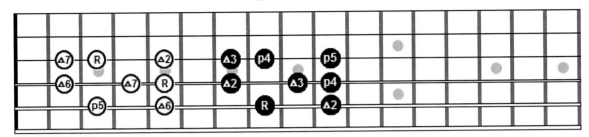

Now it is all right there within easy reach. If we go back and forth between the shapes on both string sets, our palette suddenly opens up wide.

The next few exercises will just a small sampling of some of what you can do—feel free to explore as much as you can.

Exercise #1 (mixed modes)

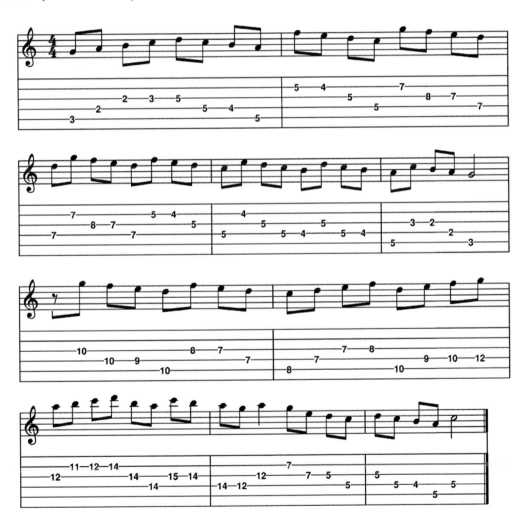

Exercise #2

Exercise #3

THE PHRYGIAN MODE

The third mode of the major scale is the Phrygian mode. The Phrygian mode is built upon the third scale degree, and it has a distinctly Flamenco-ish sound when it is played against the tonic minor. However, in diatonic applications, where it is played over the iii7 chord (Mediant 7th chord), it sounds very diatonic.

The main qualities of the Phrygian mode are that it's a minor scale with a minor 2nd, minor 6th and minor 7th. The minor 2nd gives it its exotic flavor.

E Phrygian mode

The E Phrygian has all the same notes as the C Major scale.

The Phrygian mode contains two Phrygian tetrachords (like the others, built from the tonic and the 5th), which makes it easier to remember and to find on the fretboard. Once you have memorized the shapes, it is as simple as the Ionian or Dorian modes. Here is a look at the two shapes we will be using:

Phrygian Tetrachord shapes (both string sets)

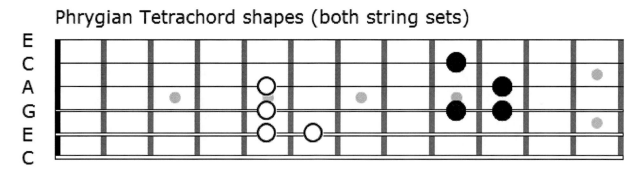

Note: the diagram above does not indicate any specific scale—it is a random example intended only to show to shapes.

PHRYGIAN TETRACHORDS
(string set 2, 3, 4)

E Phrygian mode

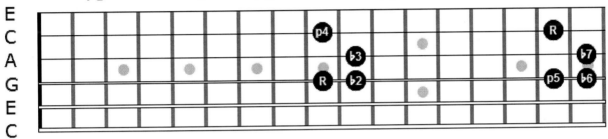

B Phrygian mode

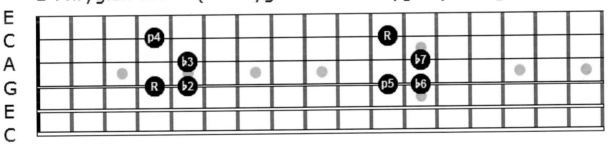

F# Phrygian mode

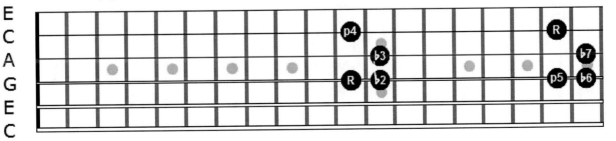

42

C# Phrygian mode

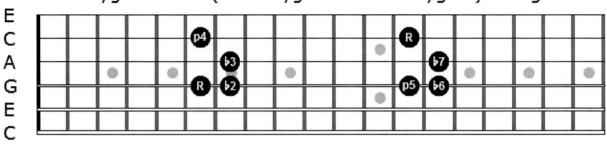

G# Phrygian mode

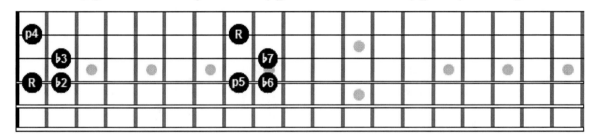

D# Phrygian mode

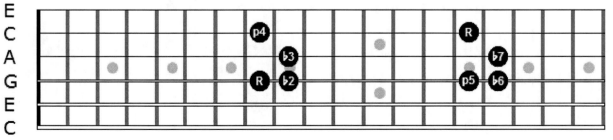

A# Phrygian mode

Bb Phrygian mode

A# (Bb) Phrygian mode (A# (Bb) Phrygian + E# (F) Phrygian) strings 234

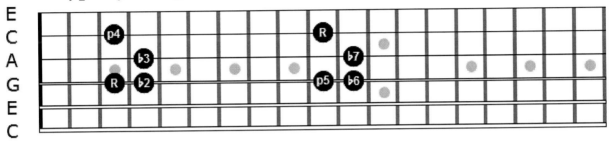

F Phrygian mode

F Phrygian mode (F Phrygian + C Phrygian) strings 234

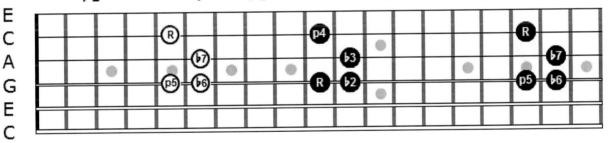

C Phrygian mode

C Phrygian mode (C Phrygian + G Phrygian) strings 234

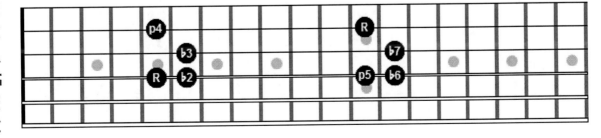

G Phrygian mode

G Phrygian mode (G Phrygian + D Phrygian) strings 234

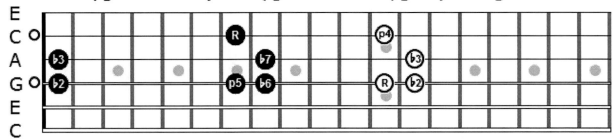

D Phrygian mode

D Phrygian mode (D Phrygian + A Phrygian) strings 234

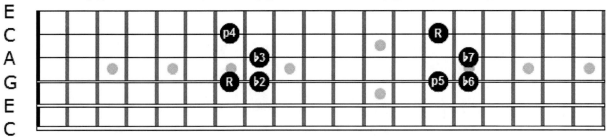

A Phrygian mode

A Phrygian mode (A Phrygian + E Phrygian) strings 234

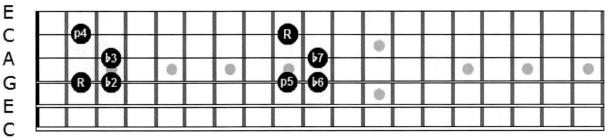

PHRYGIAN TETRACHORDS
(string set 3, 4, 5)

E Phrygian mode

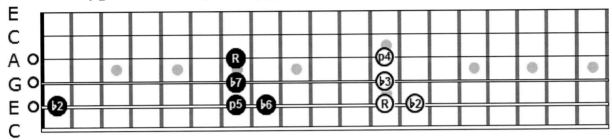

E Phrygian mode (E Phrygian + B Phrygian) strings 345

B Phrygian mode

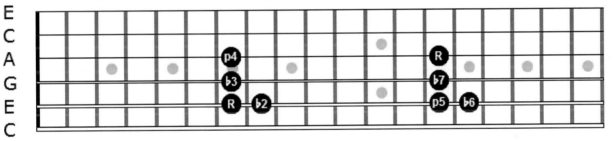

B Phrygian mode (B Phrygian + F# Phrygian) strings 345

F# Phrygian mode

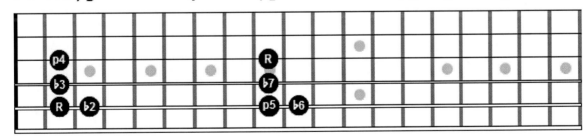

F# Phrygian mode (F# Phrygian + C# Phrygian) strings 345

C# Phrygian mode

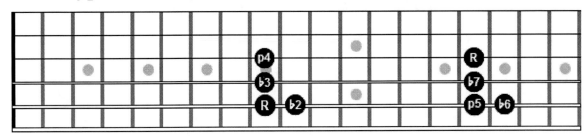

G# Phrygian mode

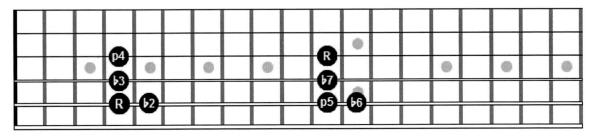

D# Phrygian mode

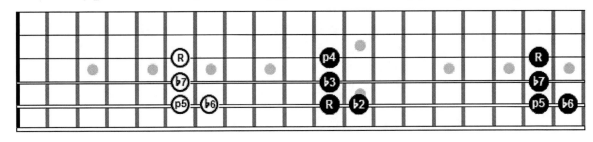

A# Phrygian mode or Bb Phrygian mode

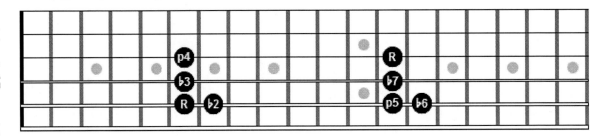

F Phrygian mode

F Phrygian mode (F Phrygian + C Phrygian) strings 345

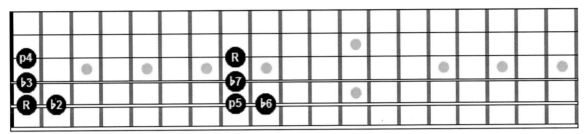

C Phrygian mode

C Phrygian mode (C Phrygian + G Phrygian) strings 345

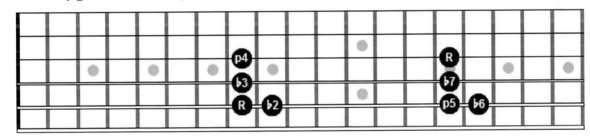

G Phrygian mode

G Phrygian mode (G Phrygian + D Phrygian) strings 345

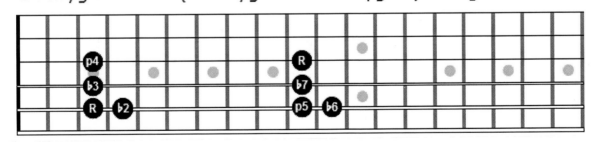

D Phrygian mode

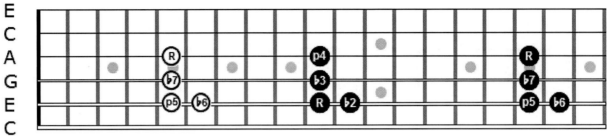

D Phrygian mode (D Phrygian + A Phrygian) strings 345

A Phrygian mode

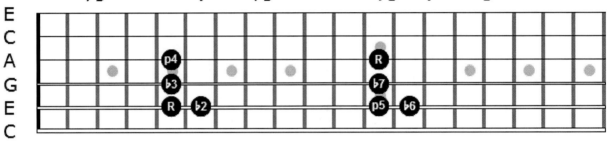

A Phrygian mode (A Phrygian + E Phrygian) strings 345

THE LYDIAN MODE

The Lydian mode is built from the 4th degree of the major scale, and it is the first of the modes we are encountering with two different tetrachord shapes. The Lydian mode is a major scale, but the difference between it and the tonic major scale is the #4 degree. The first tetrachord is a Lydian shape, and the second tetrachord the Ionian shape. An interesting point is that the second tetrachord (the Ionian) is the tonic major, so in the case of the F Lydian below, the Ionian tetrachord would be C, the parent tonic.

F Lydian mode

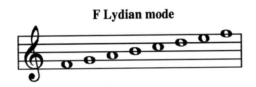

The Lydian harmony, the Subdominant Maj7 chord, or the M7#11 chord, is a very consonant chord that works not only in the function of a IVM7 chord, but also as a tonic chord, IM7#11. However, the music has to be tolerant of that sound, and much of popular music is not. An exception is when you encounter slash chords, such as D/C or A/G, where the first letter indicates the triad and the second indicates the bass note it is to be played over.

Lydian Tetrachord shapes (both string sets)

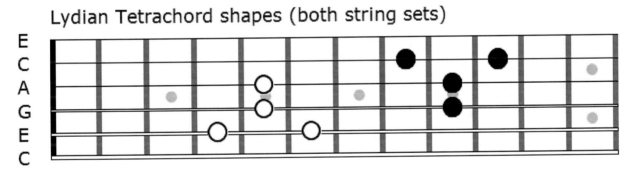

As you can see, the tetrachord shapes on the two string sets are actually mirror images of each other The most important property of the Lydian tetrachord is the fact that it is composed of three whole steps.

THE LYDIAN MODE
LYDIAN + IONIAN TETRACHORDS
(string set 2, 3, 4)

F Lydian mode

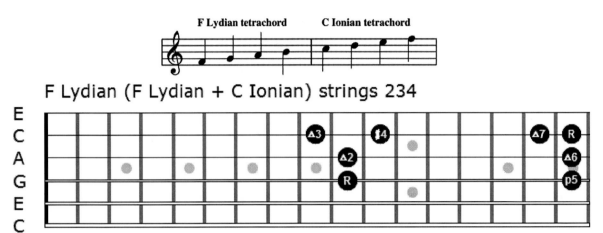

C Lydian mode

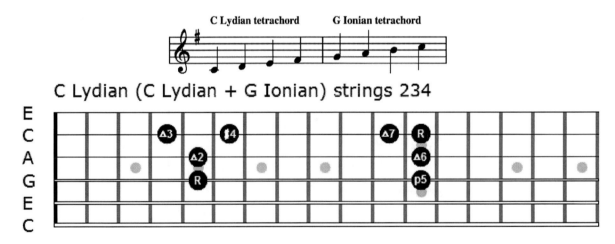

G Lydian mode

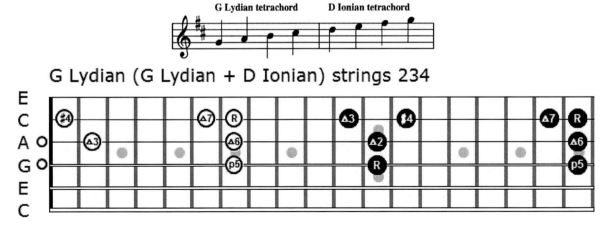

Note the unusual shape with open strings.

D Lydian mode

D Lydian (D Lydian + A Ionian) strings 234

A Lydian mode

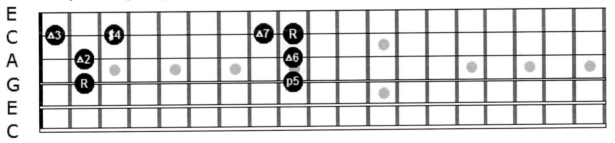

A Lydian (A Lydian + E Ionian) strings 234

E Lydian mode

E Lydian (E Lydian + B Ionian) strings 234

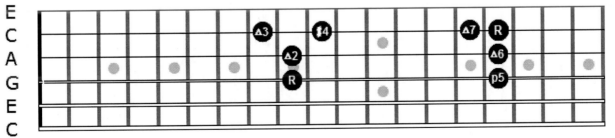

B Lydian mode

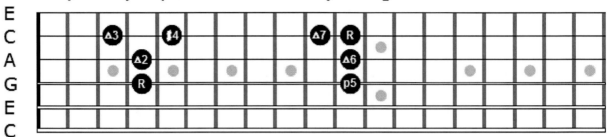

Gb Lydian mode

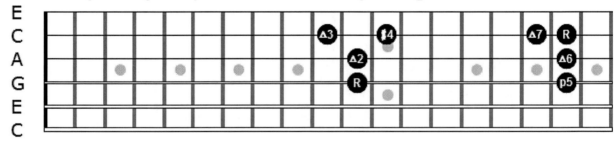

Db Lydian mode

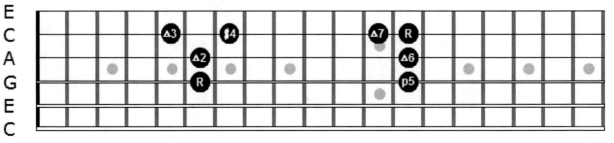

Ab Lydian mode

Ab Lydian (Ab Lydian + Eb Ionian) strings 234

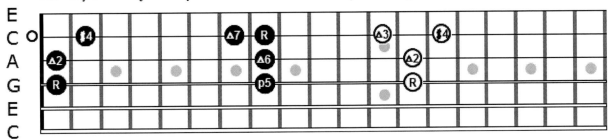

Eb Lydian mode

Eb Lydian (Eb Lydian + Bb Ionian) strings 234

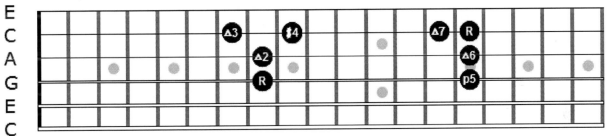

Bb Lydian mode

Bb Lydian (Bb Lydian + F Ionian) strings 234

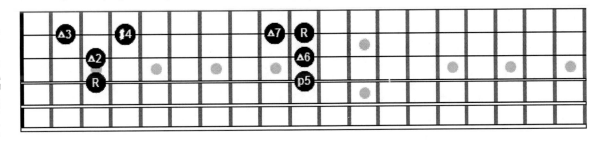

THE LYDIAN MODE
LYDIAN + IONIAN TETRACHORDS
(string set 3, 4, 5)

F Lydian mode

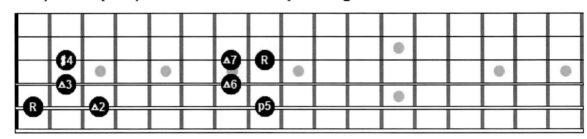

C Lydian mode

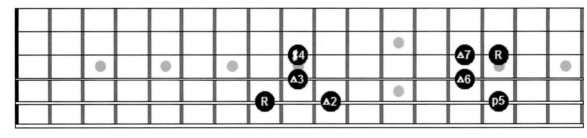

G Lydian mode

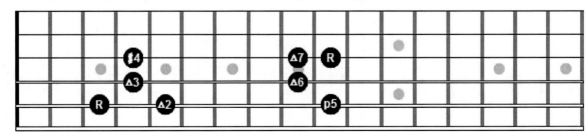

D Lydian mode

D Lydian (D Lydian + A Ionian) strings 345

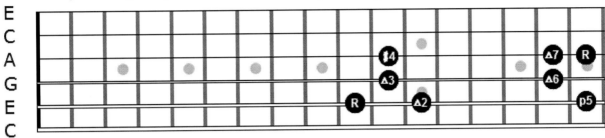

A Lydian mode

A Lydian (A Lydian + E Ionian) strings 345

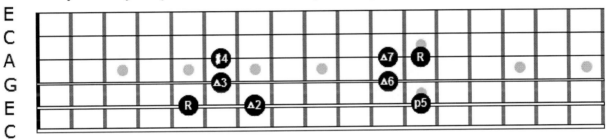

E Lydian mode

E Lydian (E Lydian + B Ionian) strings 345

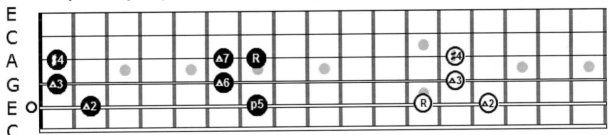

B Lydian mode

B Lydian (B Lydian + F# Ionian) strings 345

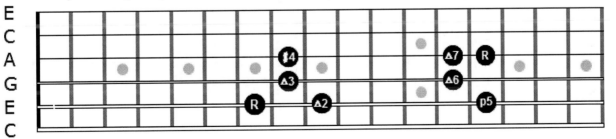

Gb Lydian mode

Gb Lydian (Gb Lydian + Db Ionian) strings 345

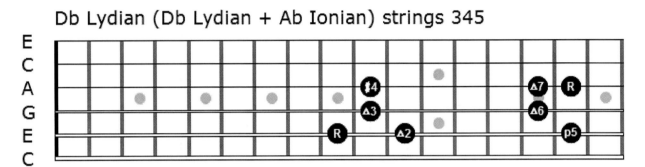

Db Lydian mode

Db Lydian (Db Lydian + Ab Ionian) strings 345

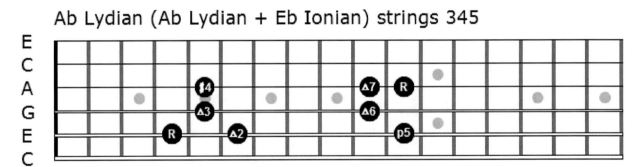

Ab Lydian mode

Ab Lydian (Ab Lydian + Eb Ionian) strings 345

Eb Lydian mode

Eb Lydian (Eb Lydian + Bb Ionian) strings 345

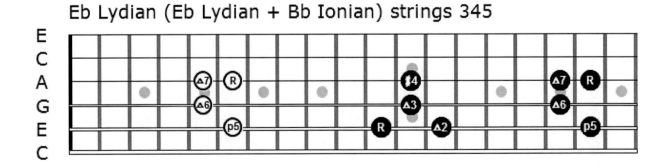

Bb Lydian mode

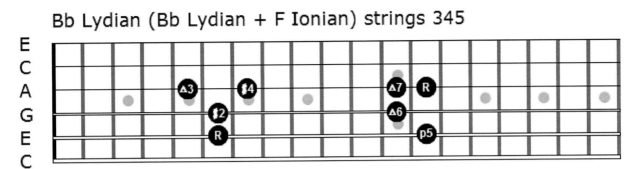

Connecting the tetrachords

We have now covered all of the tetrachord shapes in a diatonic scale, so it is possible to see how these pieces fit together. The Mixolydian, Aeolian, and Locrian modes offer no new shapes, but their importance lies in the harmonic scheme of things.

Let's look at what we've got thus far (we will focus our energies here in the key of A, which provides us with plenty of neck real estate):

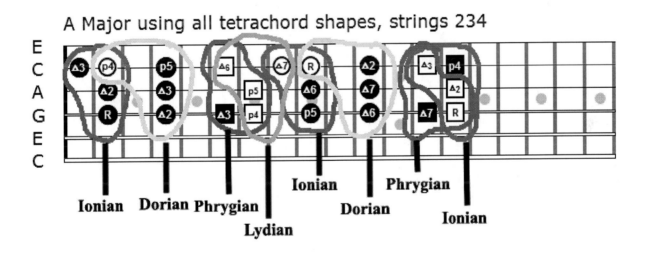

The white notes above indicate shared notes between 2 tetrachords. Rather than just look like a bunch of notes on the neck, you can you the logic in the shapes and how easy it is to navigate them. The only important consideration is knowing where your chord tones are and trying to make them your target on strong beats, or in appropriate places in your phrases.

You can see the obvious pattern: Ionian, Dorian, Phrygian, Lydian, Ionian, Dorian Phrygian. Memorize that pattern backwards and forwards and learn how to make the connection between the scale degrees and the tetrachords, and you have a bounty of choices.

It is so important to recognize at this point that just because we learned that each is built from two other tetrachords does not mean we can't play any of the other tetrachords in the diatonic scale over it! **All of the diatonic tetrachords are interchangeable!**

To further elaborate on the previous point, I will again define the relationship between the modes and the parent tonic: a major scale can exist as a mode in seven different tonal centers (one for each of its scale degrees). So, for example, the C major scale exists as modes in seven keys as well: C (Ionian), D (Dorian), E (Phrygian), F (Lydian), G (Mixolydian), A (Aeolian) and B (Locrian)—in essence, all of these modes are the C scale. However, in analyzing a chord structure for improvising, to simply say "Play the C Major scale" over any functional chord related to the C scale is doing an injustice to the music, as we want to be able to define the chord tones.

Here is a look at the tetrachord shapes on string set 3, 4, and 5:

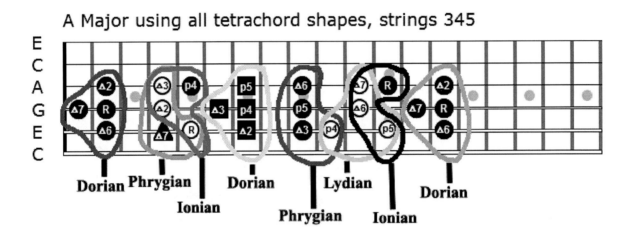

So, we begin to make these connections now and the light bulb turns on in our mind. It's it this time that a reality check is in good order, because it can become a little too easy to get overly ambitious. It is best to take this one step at a time and let your mind come to grips with the shapes and with the breakdown of the scales into modes.

The best way to do this is to play music.

THE MIXOLYDIAN MODE

The fifth mode of the major scale is the Mixolydian mode. It is also referred to as the Dominant scale, because of the flatted 7th.

G Mixolydian

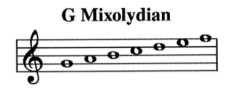

The relationship between the tonic and the V7, or dominant chord, is the most important relationship in Western music. V7 equals tension; I equals resolution. The 3rd degree of the Mixolydian mode is the leading tone, or 7th, of the Major scale, and it has a strong tendency to resolve to the tonic. In fact, as you will see later, there is a strong relationship between the V7 and the vii°7, or the half-diminished 7th, because they both contain a diminished triad—degrees 7, 9 and 11 of the tonic major.

Getting back to the importance of the V7 chord, each diatonic scale only contains one dominant chord, so if in a song you see a dominant 7th chord that isn't the V7 of the tonic key, we have what is called a *secondary dominant chord*. It's basically a fancy term for a borrowed chord that has a tendency to resolve to a chord other than the tonic. Often, you'll hear secondary dominants used in Swing tunes, like "Sweet Georgia Brown", where it cycles through secondary dominants until finally arriving at the tonic. In the event we encounter secondary dominants, we simply adopt the tonality of the secondary dominant's parent key temporarily. Having a good grasp of the tetrachord shapes in all keys will make it easier for you to navigate through those changes without having to play stale and convenient licks.

At the end of this chapter, we will begin connecting the modes and tetrachords we've covered both vertically and horizontally on the neck, and you will begin to see how all the hard work you've put in has made a difference.

MIXOLYDIAN MODE
IONIAN + DORIAN TETRACHORDS
(string set 2, 3, 4)

G Mixolydian mode

G Ionian tetrachord | D Dorian tetrachord

G Mixolydian (G Ionian + D Dorian) strings 234

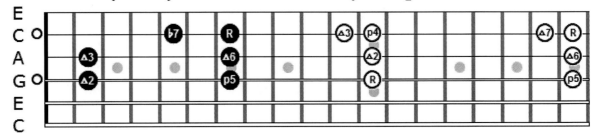

D Mixolydian mode

D Ionian tetrachord | A Dorian tetrachord

D Mixolydian (D Ionian + A Dorian) strings 234

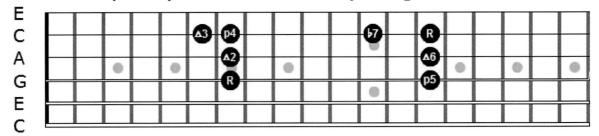

A Mixolydian mode

A Ionian tetrachord | E Dorian tetrachord

A Mixolydian (A Ionian + E Dorian) strings 234

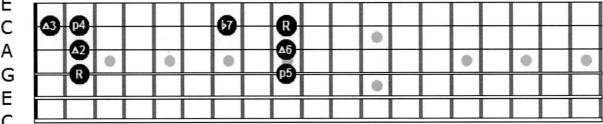

E Mixolydian mode

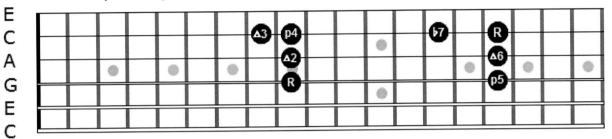

B Mixolydian mode

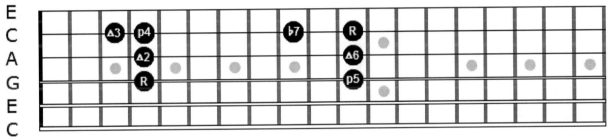

F# Mixolydian mode

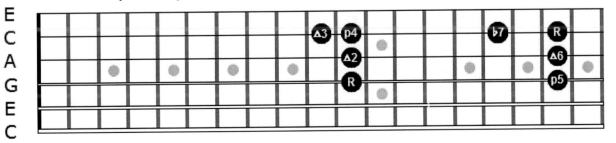

C# Mixolydian mode   or Db Mixolydian mode

C# (Db) Mixolydian (C# (Db) Ionian + G# (Ab) Dorian) strings 234

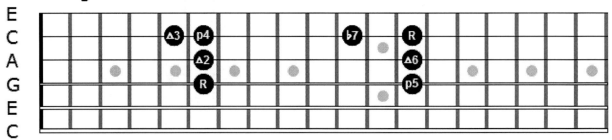

Ab Mixolydian mode

Ab Mixolydian (Ab Ionian + Eb Dorian) strings 234

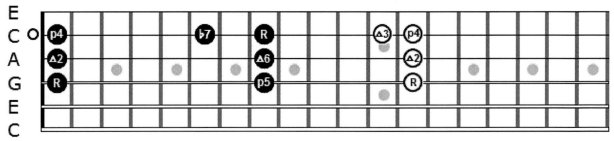

Eb Mixolydian mode

Eb Mixolydian (Eb Ionian + Bb Dorian) strings 234

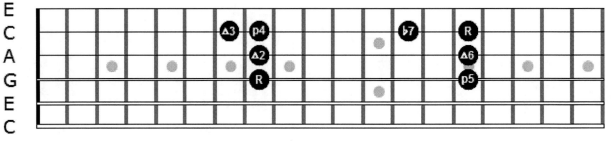

Bb Mixolydian mode

Bb Mixolydian (Bb Ionian + F Dorian) strings 234

F Mixolydian mode

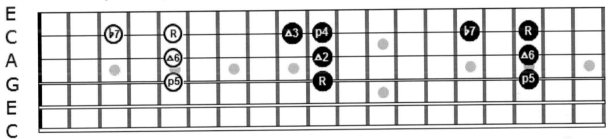

F Mixolydian (F Ionian + C Dorian) strings 234

C Mixolydian mode

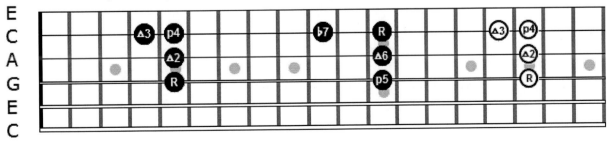

C Mixolydian (C Ionian + G Dorian) strings 234

MIXOLYDIAN MODE
IONIAN + DORIAN TETRACHORDS
(string set 3, 4, 5)

G Mixolydian mode

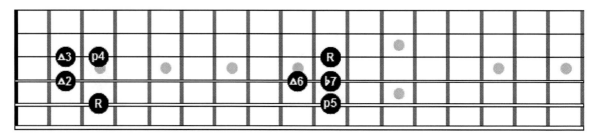

D Mixolydian mode

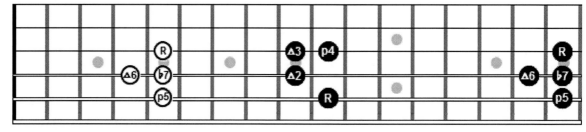

A Mixolydian mode

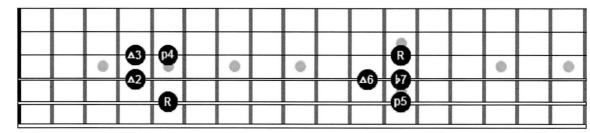

E Mixolydian mode

E Mixolydian (E Ionian + B Dorian) strings 345

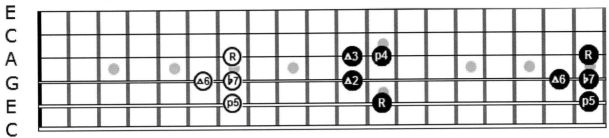

B Mixolydian mode

B Mixolydian (B Ionian + F# Dorian) strings 345

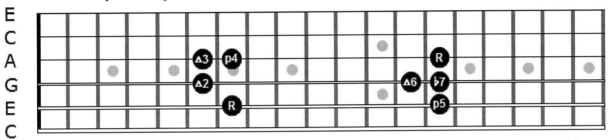

F# Mixolydian mode

F# Mixolydian (F# Ionian + C# Dorian) strings 345

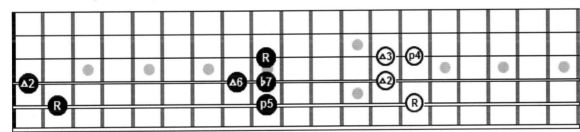

C# Mixolydian mode or Db Mixolydian mode

C# (Db) Mixolydian (C# (Db) Ionian + G# (Ab) Dorian) strings 345

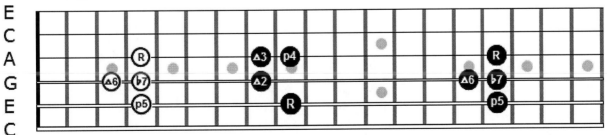

Ab Mixolydian mode

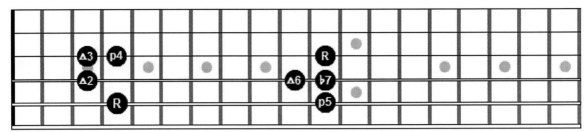

Eb Mixolydian mode

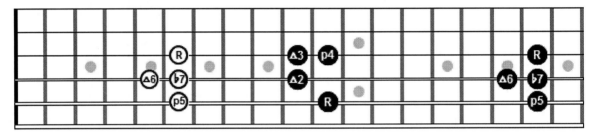

Bb Mixolydian mode

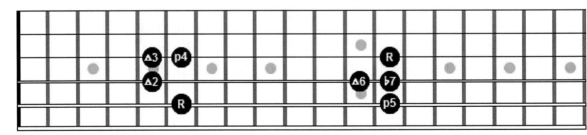

F Mixolydian mode

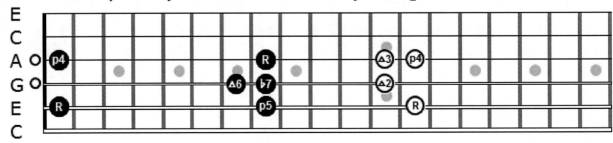

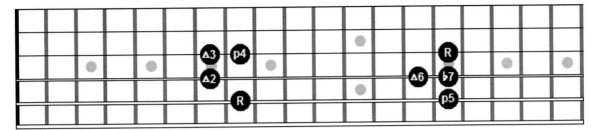

C Mixolydian (C Ionian + G Dorian) strings 345

THE AEOLIAN MODE

The Aeolian mode is the sixth mode of the major scale, and is also the relative minor or natural minor to the tonic. As a minor scale, it is weak because of its lack of a dominant V chord—the v chord in the key of A Minor is E minor, which has a weak tendency toward resolution. This was remedied with the use of the Harmonic and Melodic Minor scales which, because of their major 7th degrees, provide the V7 chord. However, there are still many examples of music which uses the Aeolian mode

A Aeolian

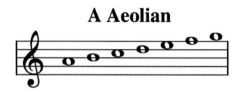

The Aeolian mode is built from a combination of a Dorian tetrachord and a Phrygian tetrachord. This pairing gives us the minor 3rd, minor 6th, and minor 7th degrees. It is a very conservative and somewhat uninteresting sound. The Dorian mode is often used instead of the Aeolian mode as a tonic minor, because of the natural 6th degree.

AEOLIAN MODE
DORIAN + PHRYGIAN TETRACHORDS
(string set 2, 3, 4)

A Aeolian mode

A Dorian tetrachord   E Phrygian tetrachord

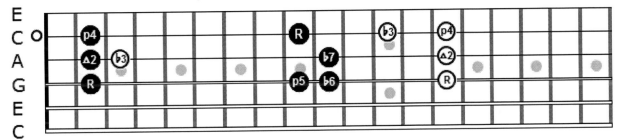

E Aeolian mode

E Dorian tetrachord   B Phrygian tetrachord

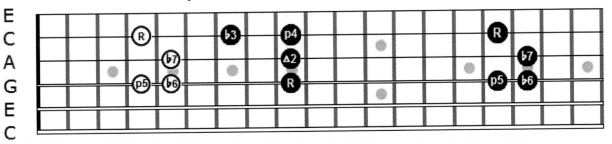

B Aeolian mode

B Aeolian mode (B Dorian + F# Phrygian) strings 234

F# Aeolian mode

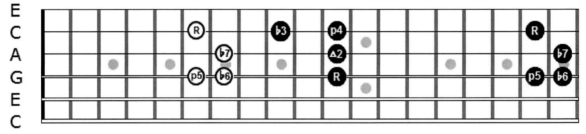

F# Aeolian mode (F# Dorian + C# Phrygian) strings 234

C# Aeolian mode

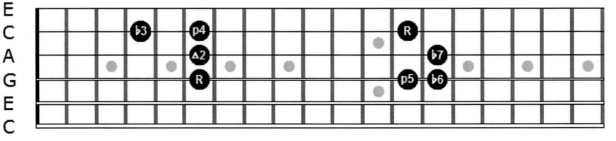

C# Aeolian mode (C# Dorian + G# Phrygian) strings 234

71

G# Aeolian mode

G# Dorian tetrachord   D# Phrygian tetrachord

G# Aeolian mode (G# Dorian + D# Phrygian) strings 234

D# Aeolian mode

D# Dorian tetrachord   A# Phrygian tetrachord

or

Eb Aeolian mode

Eb Dorian tetrachord   Bb Phrygian tetrachord

D# (Eb) Aeolian mode (D# (Eb) Dorian + A# (Bb) Phrygian) strings 234

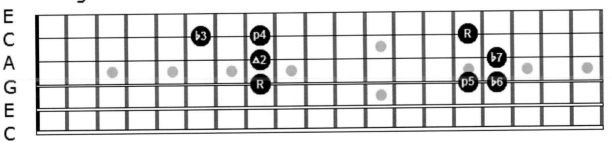

Bb Aeolian mode

Bb Aeolian mode (Bb Dorian + F Phrygian) strings 234

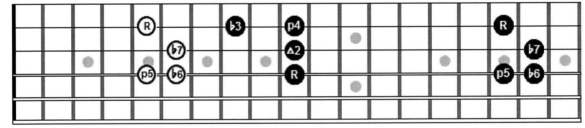

F Aeolian mode

F Aeolian mode (F Dorian + C Phrygian) strings 234

C Aeolian mode

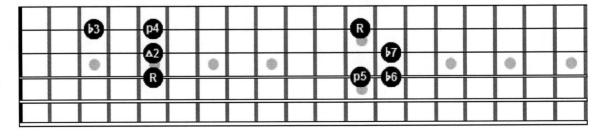

C Aeolian mode (C Dorian + G Phrygian) strings 234

G Aeolian mode

G Dorian tetrachord   D Phrygian tetrachord

G Aeolian mode (G Dorian + D Phrygian) strings 234

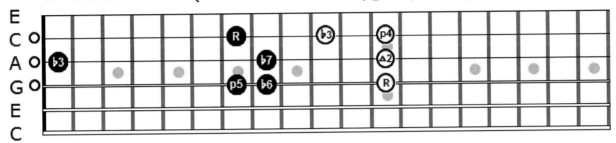

D Aeolian mode

D Dorian tetrachord   A Phrygian tetrachord

D Aeolian mode (D Dorian + A Phrygian) strings 234

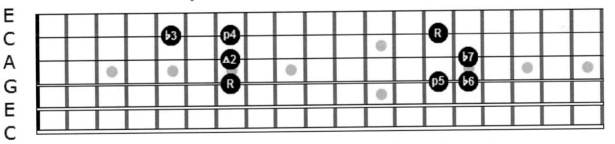

AEOLIAN MODE
DORIAN + PHRYGIAN TETRACHORDS
(string set 3, 4, 5)

A Aeolian mode

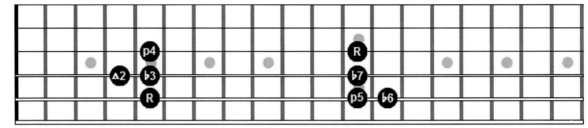

A Aeolian mode (A Dorian + E Phrygian) strings 345

E Aeolian mode

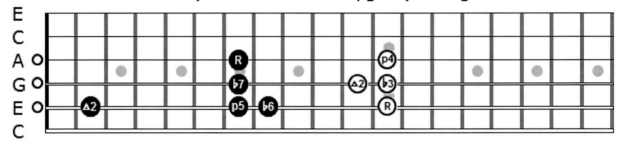

E Aeolian mode (E Dorian + B Phrygian) strings 345

B Aeolian mode

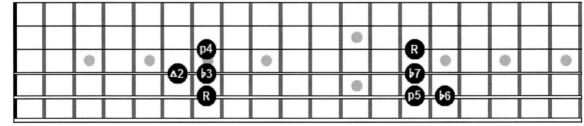

B Aeolian mode (B Dorian + F# Phrygian) strings 345

F# Aeolian mode

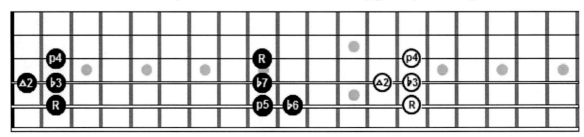

F# Aeolian mode (F# Dorian + C# Phrygian) strings 345

C# Aeolian mode

C# Aeolian mode (C# Dorian + G# Phrygian) strings 345

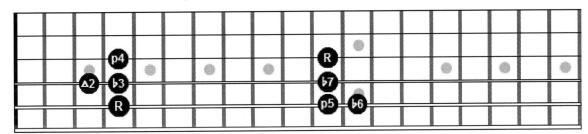

G# Aeolian mode

G# Aeolian mode (G# Dorian + D# Phrygian) strings 345

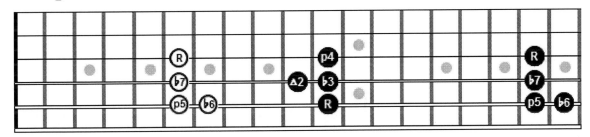

D# Aeolian mode or Eb Aeolian mode

D# (Eb) Aeolian mode (D# (Eb) Dorian + A# (Bb) Phrygian) strings 345

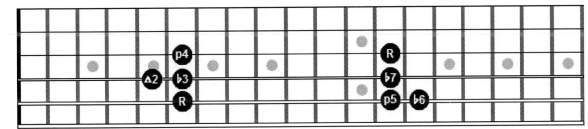

Bb Aeolian mode

Bb Aeolian mode (Bb Dorian + F Phrygian) strings 345

F Aeolian mode

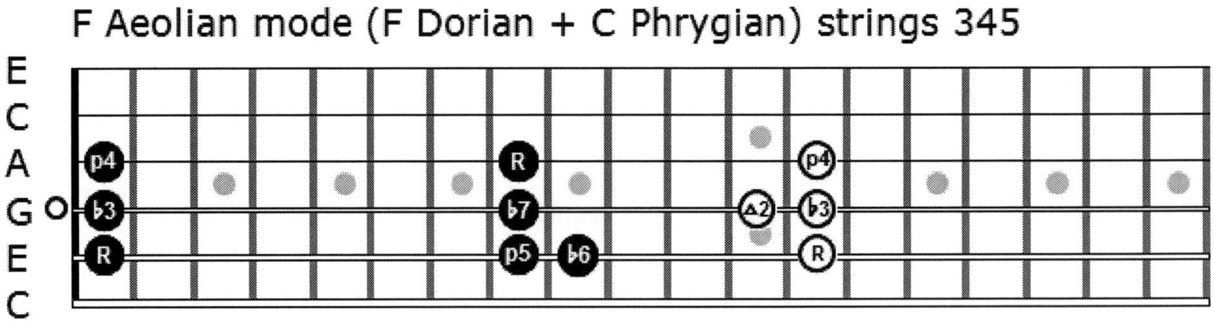

F Aeolian mode (F Dorian + C Phrygian) strings 345
E
C
A
G
E
C

C Aeolian mode

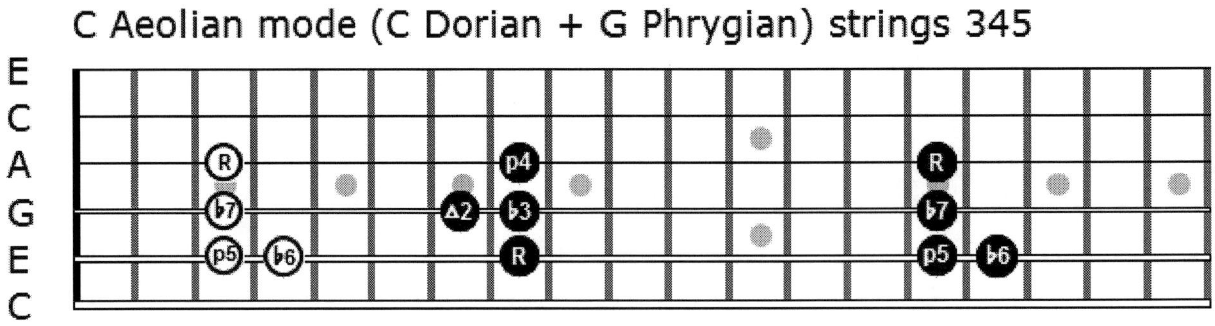

C Aeolian mode (C Dorian + G Phrygian) strings 345
E
C
A
G
E
C

G Aeolian mode

G Aeolian mode (G Dorian + D Phrygian) strings 345
E
C
A
G
E
C

D Aeolian mode

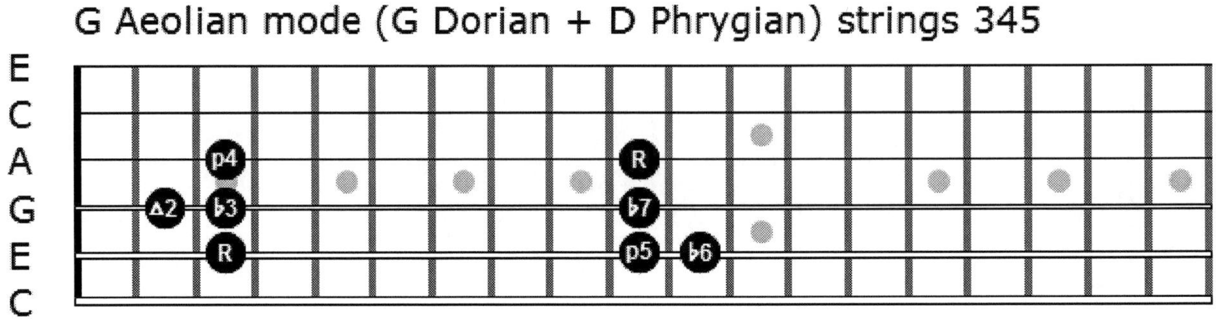

D Aeolian mode (D Dorian + A Phrygian) strings 345
E
C
A
G
E
C

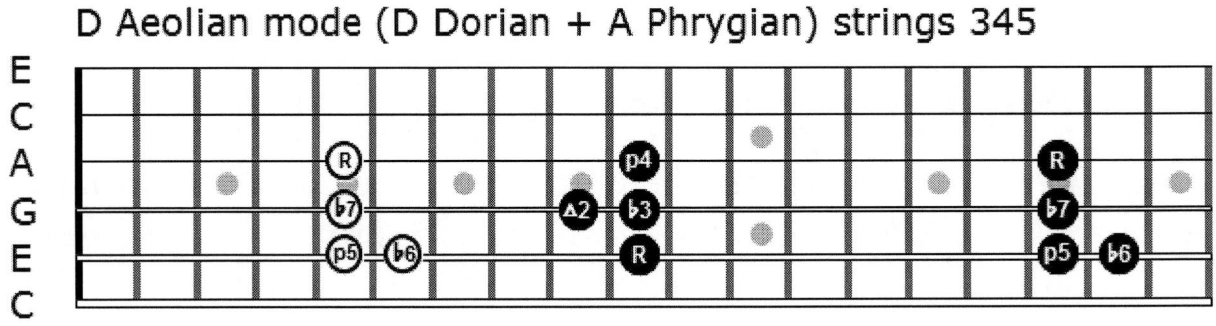

THE LOCRIAN MODE

The Locrian mode is the seventh and final mode of the Major scale. It is a minor scale with a flatted 2nd, flatted 5th and flatted 7th. In tetrachords, the Locrian consists of the Phrygian tetrachord (lower) and the Lydian tetrachord (upper). The tonic chord of the Locrian mode is a diminished triad, making the Locrian mode very unstable and giving the feeling that it should resolving to something else. The Locrian is also the only mode with a tritone between the root and the 5th degree. Being that the 5th of the mode is flatted, there is only a semitone between the upper and lower tetrachords, and the roots of the tetrachords are a tritone apart. The Lydian tetrachord begins on the flatted 5th and, with its three consecutive whole tones, provides quite an interesting sound.

B Locrian

The Locrian mode is particularly useful with the mi7♭5 or half-diminished chord, but you will find this mostly in minor ii-V7-i progressions, which also requires the use of either the Harmonic or Melodic Minor scale, which are not within the scope of this volume. If we play the Locrian mode over a CM7 chord, it simply sounds like the C Major scale; however, when played over a Bmi7♭5, that's when you'll hear the magic of the mode.

LOCRIAN MODE
PHRYGIAN + LYDIAN TETRACHORDS
(string set 2, 3, 4)

B Locrian mode

B Phrygian tetrachord   **F Lydian tetrachord**

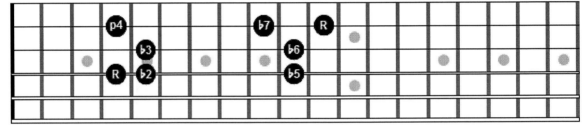

B Locrian mode (B Phrygian + F Lydian) strings 234

F# Locrian mode

F# Phrygian tetrachord   **C Lydian tetrachord**

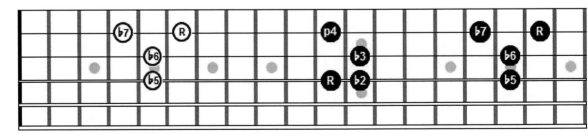

F# Locrian mode (F# Phrygian + C Lydian) strings 234

C# Locrian mode

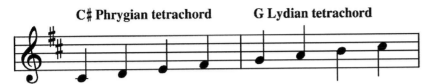

C# Locrian mode (C# Phrygian + G Lydian) strings 234

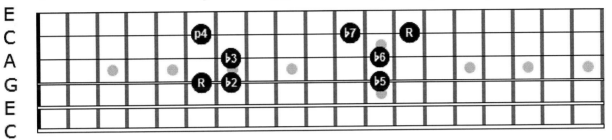

G# Locrian mode

G# Locrian mode (G# Phrygian + D Lydian) strings 234

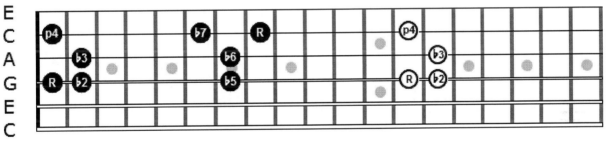

D# Locrian mode

D# Locrian mode (D# Phrygian + A Lydian) strings 234

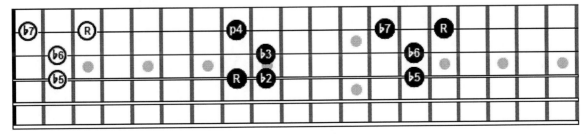

A# Locrian mode

A‡ Phrygian tetrachord　　**E Lydian tetrachord**

A# Locrian mode (A# Phrygian + E Lydian) strings 234

E# Locrian mode

E‡ Phrygian tetrachord　　**B Lydian tetrachord**

or

F Locrian mode

F Phrygian tetrachord　　**C♭ Lydian tetrachord**

E# (F) Locrian mode (E# (F) Phrygian + B (Cb) Lydian) strings 234

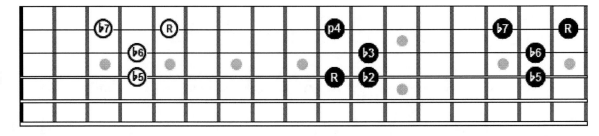

C Locrian mode

C Phrygian tetrachord   **Gb Lydian tetrachord**

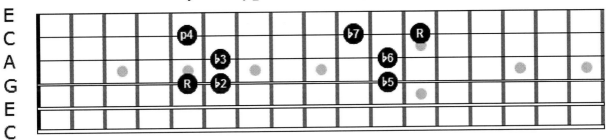

C Locrian mode (C Phrygian + Gb Lydian) strings 234

G Locrian mode

G Phrygian tetrachord   **Db Lydian tetrachord**

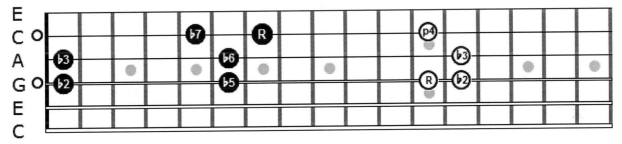

G Locrian mode (G Phrygian + Db Lydian) strings 234

D Locrian mode

D Phrygian tetrachord   **Ab Lydian tetrachord**

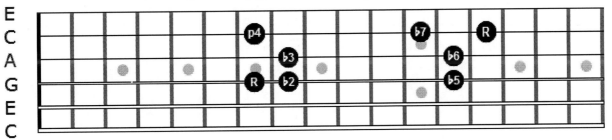

D Locrian mode (D Phrygian + Ab Lydian) strings 234

A Locrian mode

A Phrygian tetrachord   Eb Lydian tetrachord

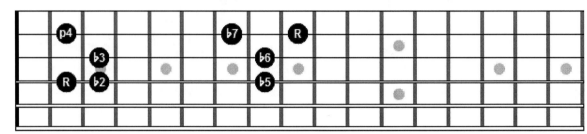

E Locrian mode

E Phrygian tetrachord   Bb Lydian tetrachord

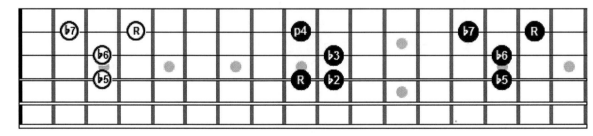

LOCRIAN MODE
PHRYGIAN + LYDIAN TETRACHORDS
(string set 3, 4, 5)

B Locrian mode

B Locrian mode (B Phrygian + F Lydian) strings 345

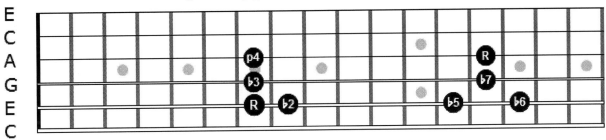

F# Locrian mode

F# Locrian mode (F# Phrygian + C Lydian) strings 345

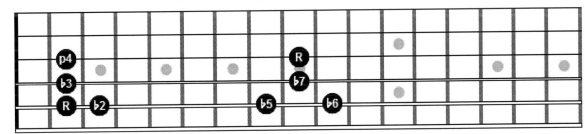

C# Locrian mode

C# Locrian mode (C# Phrygian + G Lydian) strings 345

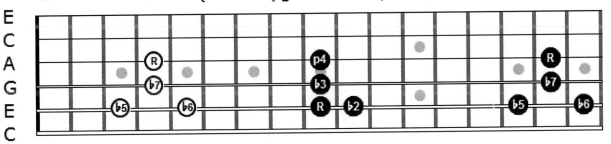

G# Locrian mode

G# Locrian mode (G# Phrygian + D Lydian) strings 345

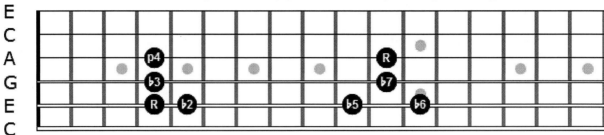

D# Locrian mode

D# Locrian mode (D# Phrygian + A Lydian) strings 345

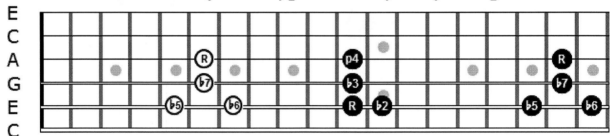

A# Locrian mode

A# Locrian mode (A# Phrygian + E Lydian) strings 345

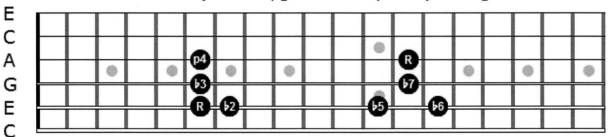

E# Locrian mode

or F Locrian mode

E# (F) Locrian mode (E# (F) Phrygian + B (Cb) Lydian) strings 345

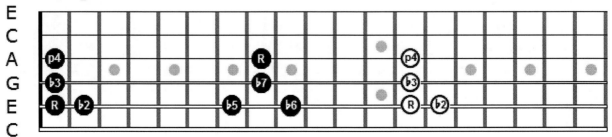

C Locrian mode

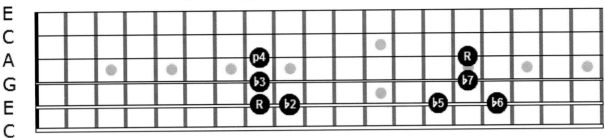

C Locrian mode (C Phrygian + Gb Lydian) strings 345

G Locrian mode

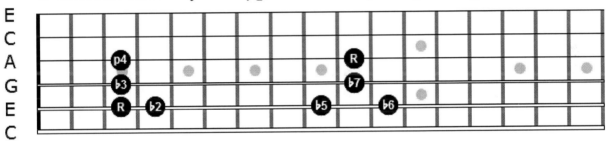

G Locrian mode (G Phrygian + Db Lydian) strings 345

D Locrian mode

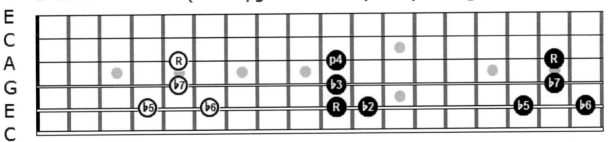

D Locrian mode (D Phrygian + Ab Lydian) strings 345

A Locrian mode

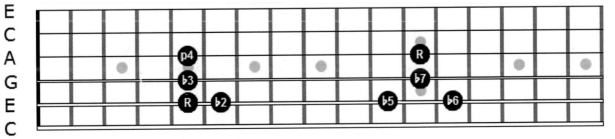

A Locrian mode (A Phrygian + Eb Lydian) strings 345

E Locrian mode

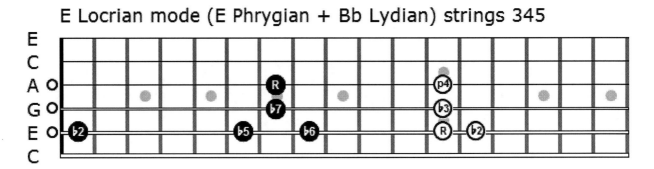

C Locrian mode (E Phrygian + Bb Lydian) strings 345

EXTENDING THE SCALES TO OTHER STRINGS

There so many variations of steel guitar tunings that it would not only be impractical, but nearly impossible to include them in a text such as this. What I've done, after much consideration, is taken the most common tuning—one which has had a standardization and continued usage probably longer than any other tuning—C6, and attempted to focus on a 4 string range where the success of the tetrachord system is most evident. We are not neglecting the other strings, but they do not fall within the convenience of the tetrachord shapes we have learned. In fact, incorporating the other strings will certainly involve a bit more bar movement—a task that, if you've learned the scales and modes in this book, really should not require much effort.

The single most important factor for proceeding is the tuning you are playing. 6 string versions of C6 are usually just C6 with 1st string E, or C6/A7, which involves tuning string 6 up to C#. The 6 string C6 with a high G is very uncommon.

For 8 string steels, the most common tunings are "high G" C6 and C13, and "high E" C6, C13 and C6/A7. The beauty of the C13 tuning is that there is an interval of a whole step between the strings tunes Bb and C, in addition to the G and A strings. This offers us more possibilities in terms using tetrachord shapes on 3-string sets. Let's take a look at how this would work for a C Major scale:

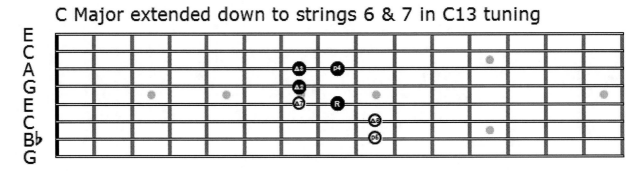

C Major extended down to strings 6 & 7 in C13 tuning

The white markers indicate the G Ionian tetrachord that we brought in (it shares the root note with the tetrachord it connects to). As you can see, it works very nicely.

If the tuning is C6 with a high E, using a G at string 8 will set us up to use the same positions as string set 234, which we've already covered. Being able to play the tetrachords an octave below in the same positions could be a very big benefit. C6 pedal players have this in their copedent, so it would be quite natural.

C Major scale using string set 678

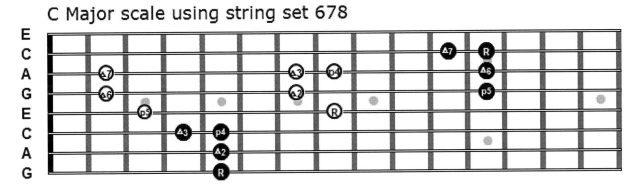

Can you see the Ionian tetrachords across the string sets? It may seem confusing now, but after you've committed the tetrachord shapes to memory it shouldn't pose any problems.

The impetus for navigating and incorporating the other strings into your scale shapes will be your own, as it is beyond the scope of this book. However, I do believe you are armed with enough information to progress forward and extend these scales to the full range of your instrument.

Other Tunings

It is also possible to utilize the Tetrachord System in numerous other tunings, so long as the tunings possess the interval of a whole step between at least two of the strings. Examples of tunings that share this property are:

A6 (E, C#, A, F#, E, C#, A, F#) – could use 2 string sets as in C6

E9 (E, B, G#, F#, D, B, G#, E)—same as string set 234

E9 pedal steel (F#, D#, G#, E, B, G#, F#, E, D, B)—could be every interesting!

As you can see, there are many possibilities to explore. Having these common threads helps to keep us from feeling completely lost and handcuffed in other tunings.

Chapter 4:
Non-Diatonic Chords
In Tonal Harmony

At this point in the book, you should already be familiar with all of the tetrachords and their relationships to the Major scales. It's been a Herculean task committing it all to memory and I'm sure you've wondered along the way whether or not it would be worth it. I think you saw enough signs along the way that it was worth it, because you persevered.

One of the most important things we've learned is that all of the modes of a Major scale are brothers and wherever one can be played, the rest of the modes of that Major scale can be played. If you are improvising over an F7 chord, not only can the F Mixolydian mode be used, but so can the G Aeolian, C Dorian, D Phrygian, A Locrian, etc., be used, because they are all the same scale when looked at within the context of diatonic harmony of the key of Bb. Knowing what we know from the Tetrachord System, we can navigate the neck moving from tetrachord to tetrachord establishing melodies, patterns, or anything else we choose. The breadth of possibilities is as wide as your imagination.

Before we move on, how well do you know your tetrachords?

1. What are the two tetrachords of D Dorian mode?

2. What are the two tetrachords of G Locrian mode?

3. What are the two tetrachords of Bb Lydian mode?

4. What is the parent scale of F Dorian?

5. Which is the only mode with tetrachords a tritone apart?

6. What is the parent scale of C# Mixolydian mode?

These are questions you should be able to answer at this point—if you can't, just stick with it and keep your focus, it will begin to stick.

Non-Diatonic Chords in Tonal Harmony

I'd like to finish this volume by talking a little about tonal harmony and how we can best put to use what we've covered outside of strict diatonic harmony. Diatonic harmony is very straightforward and easy to deal with in improvisation, because essentially we are using one scale to build the harmonies and melodies. However, a large portion of music deviates from strict *diatonicism*.

One of the most common tools in breaking free of diatonicism is called *modal interchange*. Modal interchange is simply the act of borrowing a chord/chords from a parallel tonality/modality without leaving the tonic key. What this means is that we use a chord of a different quality that is non-diatonic, but still retaining the same tonic. The most memorable example that comes to mind is the song, "*Sleepwalk*" by Santo and Johnny. Sleepwalk is essentially a I-vi-IV-V progression, except for the fact that the IV chord (F major) is actually a iv chord (F minor). Fmi is not diatonic to the key of C and therefor was borrowed. The effect of the iv chord is purely coloration and does not affect the overall tonality of the tune.

How do we determine where the iv chord was borrowed from? We have to look at F, the chord's tonic, and determine which F minor mode most closely fits the profile--in this case, most closely matches the tonality of C major. Let's examine the three minor modes of F--the Dorian, Aeolian and Phrygian:

Mode	Degrees of the modes	Common to C Major
F Dorian	F G Ab Bb C D Eb	F G C D
F Phrygian	F Gb Ab Bb C Db Eb	F C
F Aeolian	F G Ab Bb C Db Eb	F G C

You can see above that F Dorian has the most notes in common with C Major (4), so F Dorian, which is the 2nd mode of Eb Major, would probably be our first choice. For that single measure we would use the Eb scale (F Dorian in particular, so as to not lose sight of the chord tones) for improvisation. It's really such a lovely sound.

Chord Substitutions Using Modal Interchange

Now that I've brought up the subject of modal interchange, it is a necessary to talk about using chord substitutions, particularly in the case of dominant 7th chords, because the Mixolydian mode does not offer any of the altered chord extensions which are so common in today's music, particularly jazz. Our diatonic dominant 7th extended all the way up to the 13th is a beautiful chord, but it simply lacks any real color, or strong characteristics like dominant 7th chords with a b9 or b13 or both, for example. These are some of the sounds that really make ears perk up—however, the music you play must be tolerant of these harmonies, otherwise it can cause you some trouble, so use them wisely and judiciously.

One of the most common substitutions for a dominant 7th chord is the bVII7 chord, most commonly used in the "backdoor progression" iv-bVII7.

/**V7** / **I** / becomes /**iv7 - bVII7 / I** /

It is an extremely useful and colorful sound. The bVII7 provides the sound of the b9, #9 and b13. Let's say, for example, that the rhythm section is playing G7 to CMaj7—if we were use the bVII7, in this case, Bb7, we would be introducing the notes of the Eb Major scale. G is the 3rd degree of the Eb scale, which means that the Phrygian mode (built) on the 3rd degree would be the mode we would use and the modal interchange is from G7 to Gmi7. Do you see? It's the same tonic, but with a different modality.

So, to simplify, for a dominant 7th chord functioning as a V7 we can use the Phrygian mode built on the chord's tonic. It really is a simple substitution. Play this little 4-bar phrase and hear the difference between the G Mixolydian and the G Phrygian sounds:

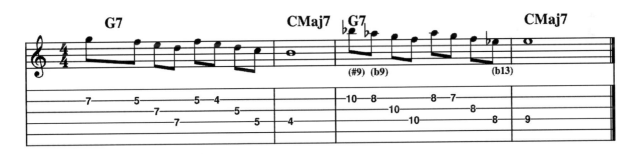

Even though the Phrygian mode is a minor mode and is missing the major 3rd of the G7 chord, it works well with dominant chords. When we begin using modes of the Harmonic Minor and Melodic Minor scales, the notes will more completely supply the chord tones and extensions, but for now, this is a nice start.

Chord Substitution Using Tritone Substitution

Another very widely used source for altered chord tones is the *tritone substitution*. A tritone substitution uses a chord that is three whole tones (a tritone) above or below the tonic. The two most important notes of a dominant chord are the 3rd and the 7th, and these two tones happen tp be a tritone apart, so simply flipping them reverses the degree in relation to the tonic (the 3rd becomes the 7th and vice versa).

In the case of tritone substitution:

/**V7** / **I** / becomes /**bII7 / I** /

The newly substituted chord is one half step above the I chord. This creates some very interesting sounds, as now we are using the sound of the Db Mixolydian mode, which is the 5th mode of the Gb Major scale.

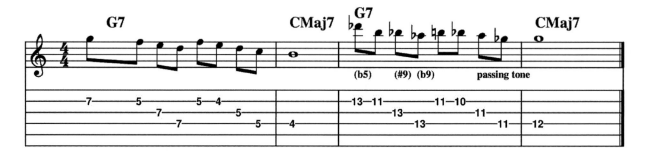

Experiment with this sound by playing all of the modes of the Gb Major scale over the G7. You must be very careful, though, since G is not present in the scale and Gb is—Gb would definitely be a note to avoid sustaining or ending a phrase on. Working out ideas ahead of time utilizing non-diatonic chords and scale can yield some fantastic results.

Secondary Dominants

The one last item I will touch on is a very important one in harmony, and that is *secondary dominants*. If you are not familiar with the term secondary dominant, it refers to a dominant 7th chord that has a diatonic root other than the IV or V and resolves to a chord other than the tonic. Every key has five secondary dominants: I7, II7, III7, VI7 and VII7. All of these dominant chords belong to other scales, but they are used to help us get from one place to another. The most basic example I can think of is a progression from the I chord to the IV chord—very often, the I chord becomes I7, which is the V7 of the IV chord. For example, we play a CMaj7 which becomes C7 which leads to FMaj7—C7 is the V7 of F.

When using secondary dominants, we temporarily use the tonality of that chord. I always tell students, "It is important to know the V of every chord you're playing at all times." The fact is, we can put the secondary dominants to use in so many ways, and they always reinforce the chord of the moment, and can really add color to a static chord. It is all about a sense of movement and resolution.

When a secondary dominant is used to reinforce a minor chord, such as in the case of III7, which is the secondary dominant of vi (III7/vi), one of the problems we are faced with in being limited to the modes of the major scale is that we don't have a leading tone, or that major 7th that would lead us to resolve to the minor. As an example, picture the progression CMaj7 to Am. What we can do is insert the secondary dominant of Am (E7) between C and Am. The E7 chord belongs to the key of A Major or the key of A Minor. The notes of the A Major scale clash against the Am, so we would turn to the A Minor scale. Again, we are limited in our choices for color tones for the E7 chord, but by using the Phrygian mode, we have the b9 which is crucial to the sound.

When the secondary dominant resolves to a chord other than a minor, we adopt the tonality of the dominant chord's parent major. A good example of this is the song *Sweet Georgia Brown*, which cycles through a number of dominant chords before resolving to the song's key center.

I've prepared one final exercise using *Sweet Georgia Brown*, and I've attempted to show how we might not only navigate through the cycle of dominants using the concept of secondary dominants, but also how we also might use modal interchange to add some flavor to the dominants as they resolve to their target chords via altered chord tones.

Displayed next to the chords are the secondary dominant functions in parentheses. The first Roman numeral refers to the dominant as the V7 and the second refers to the chord it is set to resolve to, whether diatonic or not (in the case of non-diatonic chords, you will see something like V7/biii).

Underneath the notation is the mode being used in the example. I used a Mixolydian mode to introduce each of the dominants, but just before the chord's movement to a target chord I employed some alterations to strengthen the need for resolution. I did this using modal interchange, where I would employ the Phrygian or Locrian sound associated with minor chords because of the other altered chord tones inherent to those scales (b9, #9, b13, b5). I also snuck in one very small tritone substitution in the penultimate bar.

One final note: it is important that your ideas are musical and not comprised of just running the scales. Becoming familiar with the tetrachords gives you the freedom to move in and out of them, skipping notes, using passing tones and jumping into the tetrachords of other modes. The ultimate goal is to how the freedom to express whatever it is that you want to without being confined to note choices that are convenient. It is growing beyond the perceived limitations that opens up the doors to musical expression.

I hope that this book has helped you to progress to the next level of playing and that you will continue on with a sense of curiosity and discovery—but most of all, to have some fun.

Mike

Sweet Georgia Brown

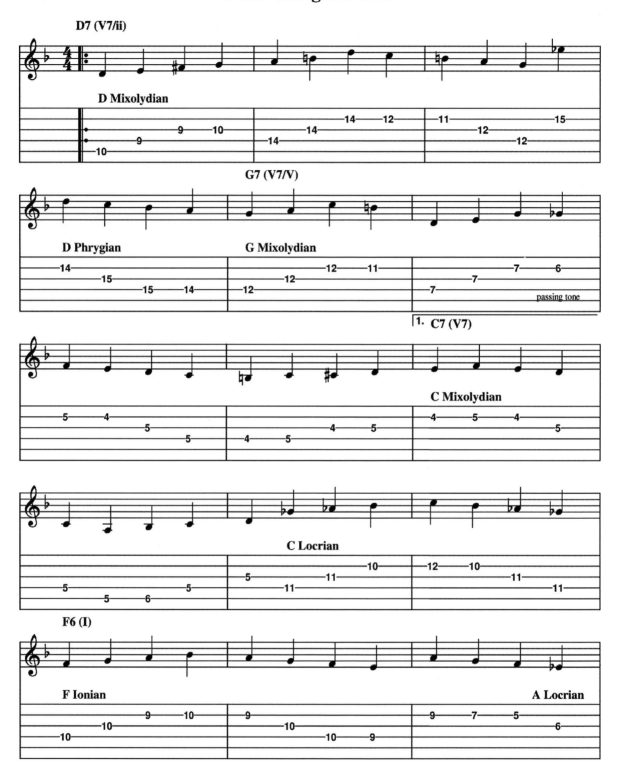

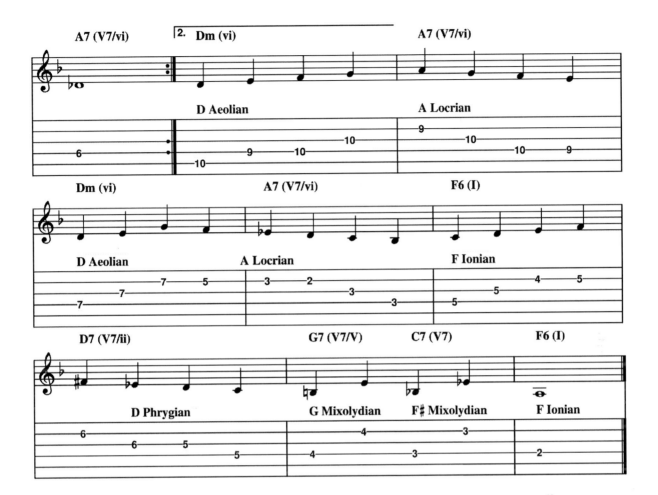